FORBIDDEN KNOWLEDGE, OR IS IT?

UNLOCKING BIBLICAL PROPHECIES AND NEW INSIGHT INTO THE LAST DAYS

EXPANDED EDITION

by D. A. Miller

JOY PUBLISHING
P.O. Box 827
San Juan Capistrano, CA 92675

Front cover design by Nira
Typesetting by Diane Fillmore

Printed in the United States of America
10 9 8 7 6 5 4

Library of Congress Cataloging-in-Publication data

Forbidden Knowledge, Or Is It?
    by D. A. Miller

    1.Miller, D. A. 2. Bible, Prophecy
Library of Congress Card # 91-76067
International Standard Book Number 0-939513-75-7

Published by
Joy Publishing
P.O. Box 827
San Juan Capistrano CA 92675

Table of Contents

PUBLISHER'S PREFACE

It is a rare occasion when an unfinished manuscript literally cries out to be published. *Forbidden Knowledge*, however, was one of those unusual manuscripts. In fact, it went to the top of the list of projects because of the urgency I felt for its message. Let me explain my reasons.

For many years, I had the concept that prophecy was something only "weirdos" studied and talked about. I distanced myself from anyone who discussed prophecy. Prophetic literature I came across seemed speculative and the speakers just added to the confusion.

Then I heard Chuck Missler, a radio Bible teacher. I listened as he revealed Scripture to me like no one ever had before. Soon, I realized that I had never heard these background details of Scripture. He showed that a very large part of the Bible is prophetic in nature. I came to see that the Bible could not be studied in its entirety without studying prophecy.

These in-depth insights began to make the Bible more clear to me. I gained a new desire to read God's Word. This interest in God's Word changed me from a man who tried to live in a Christian manner to a man who had a personal relationship with Jesus Christ.

That is why the manuscript was so important to me. The detailed background information presented in this book opens up the Scriptures in a special way. I pray that the Holy Spirit will lead you to truth and understanding.

Woody Young, Publisher

FOREWORD

Bible prophecy, especially eschatology (the study of "the last things"), has suffered greatly at the hands of both its enthusiasts and its detractors—the enthusiasts with their zeal for premature and unfounded conclusions; the detractors with their allegorizations and failure to regard the ancient texts with adequate diligence.

It is refreshing to experience a resurgence of interest in the literal and mystical aspects of the Scriptures. As a specialist in the information sciences for over thirty years, I have long been fascinated with the integrity of the Scriptures as a whole: sixty-six books, penned by forty authors over thousands of years—and yet evidencing an intricate design in which every textual detail, every number, every place name, all manifest careful design and diligent attention to detail.

It is in this very manner that this book explores some remarkable aspects of the Feasts of Israel—not just their historical basis and their commemorative role, but their prophetic role as well.

It is one of the tragedies of the historic Christian church that the widespread illiteracy with respect to the Tanakh (the Old Testament), as well as the general ignorance of "things Jewish," has masked from so many some of the amazing insights which God has hidden in the Torah (the first five books of Moses) with regards to His "Grand Design."

Furthermore, we have all been so badgered about the elusiveness of the "day and the hour" that we easily fall into the trap of being blindsighted by that which we can—and are instructed—to know.

Indeed, it is time for a fresh look.

Many of the perspectives and conjectures of the author will certainly meet with skepticism and disagreement, but this provocative study should challenge the reader to explore these insights further. After all, if we are "Children of the Day" (not of the Night) that day should *not* overtake *us* as a thief (1 Thessalonians 5:1-6).

Chuck Missler

AUTHOR'S ACKNOWLEDGMENTS

Words cannot express my appreciation to the kind friends (new and old) who used their time to read and critique this book. God graciously spoke to me through them. Their encouragement as well as their discerning comments brought this book, *Forbidden Knowledge*, into existence. Although I can offer no suitable recompense for their assistance, my prayer is that our wonderful Lord will greatly bless them for their contributions.

INTRODUCTION

The Word of God is indeed alive and powerful. The Holy Spirit of God does teach those who prayerfully seek truth from the pages of Scripture.

This book reflects an eighteen-year struggle to adjust some of my prophetic beliefs to the Word of God. I had been taught, and I firmly believed, that although the general times and seasons of end-time events could be known from the Scriptures, "no one could know the day nor the hour."

Forbidden Knowledge questions this traditional theological interpretation of "the day and hour" and other Scriptures thought to prohibit exact dating of end-time events.

First you'll see in this book the amazing precision of God's prophetic information in the customs and feasts of Israel. Then, two more celebrations are explored which reveal *hidden truths* about the times in which we live and which we are about to enter. Last, prompted by this enlightening information, you'll read a careful review of each Scripture and the traditional reasons that have kept us from believing we could know the "day and the hour."

In addition to three new chapters in this expanded version, you'll discover exciting new insights throughout the entire book.

SECTION I
PICTURES YES, BUT ARE THEY LABELED?

All Bible-believing Christians agree that prophecy is woven throughout the Scriptures. Everyone sees these pictures but how, specifically, does God reveal the timing of these events? Is the timing of some major events explained in the Scriptures while the arrival of other major events are purposely hidden from our view?

In this section we will examine the "date setting" phenomenon of our day as well as gaze at one of the most beautiful prophetic pictures in the Bible.

CHAPTER 1
DATE SETTERS ATTACK AGAIN

"Hear ye hear ye, Jesus is coming! Sell all that thou dost own and wait with the faithful on top of yonder mountain."

The faithful heard. They sold all their worldly goods, they traveled to yonder mountain, and they waited, and they waited, and they waited. Jesus did not come. Saddened and disillusioned, the followers lifted the hems of their white robes and descended the mountain amid the jeers of scoffing unbelievers.

Since the first century, when Jesus made His promise to return for those who placed their trust in Him, eager seekers have sought to discover the time of His arrival. Again and again earnest followers trusted in the projected dates only to be bitterly disappointed when Jesus did not appear.

A typical example of this phenomenon grew from the teachings of William Miller. He made his splash in the pond of prophetic history by predicting Christ's visible return in 1843, but later postponed the date to October 22, 1844. Thousands of eager followers of this guide sold all their belongings, gathered together on the special date, and waited in zealous anticipation. Those vying for the front row "climbed to the tops of trees,"[1] presumably so they would be taken first. Great disillusionment followed when the day came and left without the appearing of Christ.

Reactions to Predictions

Looking back over the centuries at the disheartened folks, who trusted the wisdom of numerous predictions, brings sadness. This sadness comes first from the realization that scores of people blindly followed the "enlightened" understanding of a prophetic interpreter. Often, these predictors used only the troubled events of their times as the basis for their chosen "apocalyptic" dates. Also heartbreaking are the many unbiblical **reactions** to belief in the soon coming of their Savior. One has to ask what **climbing a tree** has to do with meeting our beloved Jesus Christ?

Certainly, if at any time God actually had revealed the day of Jesus' Second Coming, the believer's reactions should have been ones of deeper commitment to serving Christ, conforming to His image, and telling others of His saving grace. Their often bizarre withdrawal from society and clinging to one another demonstrates a lack of searching the Scriptures for "the whole counsel of God." Soberly, in this twentieth century, we viewed the Jonestown massacre as an ultimate illustration of these bizarre reactions. The tragic death of nine hundred people resulted from a compelling desire to follow a leader rather than personally to search the Scriptures for truth.

Twentieth Century Rise in Predictions

As we near the end of the twentieth century, a rise in "doomsday setting" is again being heard. This increase in "date setting" is familiar. Historically, mankind has endeavored to tie in biblical prophecy with the calendar and with world events. However, this effort always seems to increase toward the end of every century as well as during times of disaster and social upheavals.

The editors of *The Encyclopedia of Religion* list one idea for this rise in "end time" interest: "The historical myth[a] persists because it seems to many that the year 2000 will be truly millennial. The discovery of the Dead Sea Scrolls since 1947 has underscored the contention, popularized by Albert Schweitzer in 1906, that eschatological[b] hope was vital at the time of apostolic Christianity and should therefore be a part of all true Christian belief. Israel's statehood in 1948 and its 1967 reunification of Jerusalem have convinced fundamentalist Christians of the nearness of the Second Coming, for which a principal sign is the Jew's return to Zion."[2]

Time magazine states that its senior writer, Otto Friedrich, refers to this phenomenon in a book he authored. "In his meditation on history, *The End of the World*, solemn predictions of earth's final days have accompanied natural and man-made catastrophes down through the ages, from the sack of Rome to the Nazi Holocaust. This century's military technology has given new power to those primoral fears and illusions."[3]

"The world is headed for 'Apocalypse soon'" begins a story in *US News and World Report*. The article relates the swelling sound of prophetic voices prompted by world events, particularly in the Middle East. "This isn't just the talk of a handful of charlatans, exhorting naive followers

---

[a] From this description of the biblical teaching of the Millennium, one must assume this editor lives with no expectancy of the coming of Jesus.

[b] Study of last or final things, particularly related to the Bible.

to sell their possessions and flee to the mountains. It is a message increasingly being heard from the pulpits and airwaves of mainstream Christian evangelists and resonantly striking a chord among tens of thousands of conservative Christians." This writer continues by mentioning Billy Graham's warning that "there are 'spiritual forces at work' in the Persian Gulf confrontation. 'History has gone full circle, and we are coming back to these [Bible] lands.'"[4]

Indeed, the twentieth century has been saturated with predictions of impending doom, messiahs and utopian world peace. The seventies and the eighties encountered a large share of selected dates which passed with no fulfillments. The nineties promise an explosion of prophetic forecasts.

How strange that although theologians point to specific Scriptures that forbid the knowledge of an exact date, a minority of curious seekers continue to search for this "forbidden" information.

Although respected Christian theologians, since the time of Christ, have not agreed on every detail concerning the Second Coming of Christ and the end of the world, they have concurred in one area. They have agreed that the **exact timing** of the coming of Jesus is hidden from mankind by God. Of course, cited as proof are the words of Jesus, "*No man knoweth the day and the hour.*"[a]

---

[a] Matthew 24:36; Mark 13:32

Why Do They Continue?

One does wonder why these date setters continue their hunt amid the flack coming from both conservative and liberal Christians as well as the secular world. Are they deluded? Aren't they aware of Scriptures that expressly prohibit this kind of search? Do they have any biblical ground on which to stand or are they, as some critics suggest, simply sensationalists seeking to sell books or to be noticed?

Sincere Christians know that the Bible contains many exact prophesies. The existence of prophecy is not in question but we must follow scriptural guidelines to determine the extent that **future prophetic events** can be understood.

Because of the torrent of prophetic teaching flooding over us during the end of the twentieth century, we must deal with this "dating" trend. In an effort not to damage members of the Christian body, this analysis will be done by carefully examining biblical prophesies both past and future rather than challenging individual teachers.

Prophetic Pictures

The exactness of the fulfilled prophesies concerning the first coming of Jesus (His birth, life, death, and Resurrection) have convinced Christians throughout the ages that Jesus is indeed the Messiah prophetically described in the pages of the Old Testament. Since the New Testament (as well as most of the Old) was written by Jews, much of our inquiry about prophetic events will be done from a Jewish perspective.

We will look particularly at the following question concerning the timing of future events: Since Scripture foretold precise details concerning the **first** coming of Jesus, can we expect Scriptures to reveal future world events and the timing of Jesus' **second** appearance?

This book will reveal precise information concerning future events. More importantly, it will offer scriptural freedom to look for exact times of end-time events.

In the past, followers of soothsayers reacted to prophecy in an unbiblical manner. As we hear prophecy taught today and as we consider the suggestions in this book, we must react as did the Bereans whom God commended. They knew that when anyone claimed to possess information from God, the information must be examined in light of the Scriptures as to *"whether those things were so."*[a]

As obedient Christians in a world of darkness we also must individually *"study to show thyself approved unto God, a workman that needeth not to be ashamed, rightly dividing the word of truth,"*[b] and *"be ready to answer every man that asketh a reason of the hope that is in you, with meekness and fear."*[c] We must insure that each scriptural interpretation we embrace comes from the teaching of the Holy Spirit, not just from opinions of men. At times it's tempting to rely on the studies and viewpoints of those whom we respect, as if these mortals knew all truth. However, we must continually remind ourselves that God holds each **individual** accountable for *"rightly dividing the word of truth."*[d]

---

[a] Acts 17:10, 11

[b] II Timothy 2:15

[c] I Peter 3:15

[d] II Timothy 2:15

Historic Messianic Anticipation

The belief in the soon-coming of Christ permeated Christian belief throughout the first three centuries after Christ. According to historical records, James, the half brother of Jesus, declared just before his execution, "Jesus is about to come on the clouds of heaven."

The Encyclopedia of Religion and Ethics records that noted believers Ignatius and Polycarp believed themselves to be living in the last times. They expected Christ to suddenly appear, executing judgment upon the persecutors of Christians and rewarding the faithful.

One of the early apologists[a], Justin, thought that Christ might delay His Second Coming temporarily to allow more sinners to repent, "even long enough to include some who are not yet born."

One leader in the early church, Irenaeus, agreed with the Epistle of Barnabas "in placing the end of the world and the return of Christ six thousand years after creation."[5]

A falling away in the belief of a literal Second Coming and actual one-thousand-year reign of peace by Jesus Christ resulted from Origen's introduction of an allegorical interpretation to the Scriptures. This approach to Scripture stifled interest in prophetic study and produced doubt in the relevancy and inspiration of the prophetic portions of the Bible. Until after the eleventh century, a wilful neglect of prophecy dominated the larger organizations of those who called themselves Christians.

Historically, just a few scattered students of the prophetic Scriptures maintained a belief in the literal, imminent return of Jesus. However just before the year

---

[a] A person involved in systematic defense of the divine origin and authority of Christianity.

1000, a surge of interest flowed across Christian groups. Researchers tell us that leading theologian Augustine's "identification of the Church with the ideal earthly kingdom of Christ implied that the millennium would close about A.D. 1000, and that the final coming of Christ in judgment might be expected. The approach of this date awakened a revival of interest in Second Advent hopes and for several years thereafter more or less vivid expectations were frequently entertained."[6]

In the article "Millennial Madness," Ron Rhodes refers to people caught up in this wave of millennial prospect. "Prisoners were freed yet many remained, wishing to expiate their sins before the end. As Christmas (A.D. 999) arrived, there was an outpouring of love. Stores gave away food; merchants refused payment. On December 31 the frenzy reached new heights."[7]

Sadly, as the year rolled over into 1000 with no appearance of Christ, life soon returned to normal. The euphoria of love towards one another gave way once more to a climate of self-centered existence.

From the twelfth to the twentieth centuries, eager but mistaken predictors of "end-time" dates bobbed to prominence. Each date stirred faithful, but perhaps gullible, followers. In some instances the promoters of these projected dates admonished their adherents to live in purity to prepare for the soon-expected arrival of Jesus. More commonly, however, devoted followers were deluded by these convincing "prophets" to forsake all their worldly goods and gather at some lofty or secluded place where they, "the faithful," would be the only ones invited to rise to meet the expected Savior.

Throughout history many of these seekers committed themselves to the prediction of an **exact day** for the

coming of Christ! A few of the well-known predictions
are:[8]

1. Joachim of Flores gave A.D. 1260 as the
expected return of Christ. He based this on the
1260 days listed in Revelation 12. The Crusades and
other cataclysms of his day fueled a belief in this
date.

2. Militz of Kromeriz was more conservative.
His date rested somewhere from 1365 to 1367.

3. Scottish mathematician, John Napier,
wisely gave space in his prediction. He expected
the "End" somewhere between 1688 and 1700.

4. Joseph Mede used information from
Revelation to select 1660 as the close of history.

5. Pierre Jurieu of France "sought to comfort
the Huguenots by predicting the downfall of the
Antichrist Roman Church in the year 1689."[9]

6. William Whitson boldly gave 1715, which
he changed to 1734, which he then changed to 1866!

7. J.A. Bengal concluded that a preliminary
millennium would be inaugurated in 1836.

8. Joseph Smith, well-known founder of the
Mormon church (Church of Jesus Christ of Latter-
Day Saints), told his followers in 1830 that God had
chosen him to found a community that would
constitute a present city of Zion. This city would be
ready for Christ when He set up His millennial
kingdom.[10]

9. Joseph Worlf "began prophesying that Jesus would come to the Mount of Olives in 1847. English traveler, Lady Hester Stanhope, converted to his doctrine, moved to Palestine, and established residence on the Mount of Olives. She kept two beautiful white Arabian horses in stables there. One was for Jesus to ride through the Golden Gate."[11]

10. C.T. Russell was the last great predictor of the nineteenth century. He declared 1874 as the definite date for the return of Christ and announced 1914 as the end of the world. This predictor's present-day disciples, known as Jehovah's Witnesses, now take the posture that the prophesied invisible return of Jesus Christ actually took place in 1914 but only the faithful discerned it with "eyes of understanding"!

11. Probably the most widely publicized of the twentieth century dates is September 11–13, 1988. Edgar C. Whisenant was adamant in his book, *88 Reasons The Rapture Could Be in 1988*, about the selection of these days for the Rapture of the Christian Believers. Not to be overlooked, other less outspoken prophecy teachers also placed their apples in this same-dated basket. Although some vigilant Christians immediately and openly criticized these teachers for "date setting," most of the critics waited until after the date passed with no Rapture or appearance of Jesus before they literally piggy-backed one another to ridicule the "soothsayers."

Christians Aren't the Only Predictors

Even Jewish religious leaders are picking up on the end-time fervor. This anticipation involves genuine belief that the Temple must be rebuilt now, in preparation for the soon-coming Messiah. A group of Jews faithfully prepares implements to furnish the expected Temple, while others fashion proper priestly garb for the qualified Kohens[a] who currently train for Temple service.

Some Jews actually busy themselves locating solid red-haired cows. Biblical law requires the sacrifice of a "red heifer" for the cleansing ceremony[b] in order for Temple service to be legally reinstated. Other searchers dedicated to this soon-to-come messianic time are frantically exploring special caves in Israel to try and locate the original ashes of the Red Heifer and other authentic Temple artifacts. They believe that an ancient copper scroll, found in cave number eight, specifically describes a cave where the Temple treasures were hidden just before the destruction of the Temple in A.D. 70.

Some searchers also believe these caves might be the location of the original Ark of the Covenant while others give convincing reasons why the Ark might be located in Ethiopia.[12]

The messianic fervor is fanned by reports such as this one in *The Jerusalem Post*. "Rebbe Menahem Schneerson, a beloved Lubavicher leader, stated in August of 1990, 'This year, according to a Midrash (a homiletical[c] interpretation

---

[a] Descendants of Aaron from the Jewish tribe of Levi.

[b] Numbers 8:6, 7, 19:1-22

[c] Teaching through preaching.

of the Scripture), there will be great ferment between the different states, and then a confrontation in the Gulf that will shake the world. **Then Messiah will come,** stand on the roof of the Temple, and announce to Israel: The time of your redemption has come."[13]

"What is going on in Iraq is definitely **a sign of the imminent arrival of the Messiah,**" quoted the *Miami Herald* of Rabbi Mendel Fogelman, a leader of the Israeli branch of the dynamic, modern, and yet fundamentalist, Chabad movement.[a]

Although the messianic fervor is building in the nineties, Rabbi Professor Leon Askhenazi, a Jerusalem-based Sephardi scholar, believes, "One does not just get up and start believing in a Messianic Era just because of what happens this year. I believe that the process was underway a long time ago, because the advent of Zionism signified the Ingathering of the Exiles."

Some projections for the messianic movement, mentioned in the *Post* article, include ideas such as "using 1917 and the Balfour Declaration as the starting point for the Ingathering of the Exiles." Askhenazi states, "The Book of Daniel predicted that fifty years after the Ingathering, Jerusalem will be reunified (1967), to be followed twenty-five years later by the reconstruction of the Temple."

Askhenazi "acknowledges the dangers of over-enthusiasm in making conclusions based on today's headlines. Yet he notes certain pre-messianic parallels: the war occurring at the same time as the massive Soviet/Ethiopian Aliya (the Ingathering of the Exiles) and America's role in the Gulf (there is a biblical passage noting that others will do Israel's work for her **prior to the arrival of the Messiah.**")[14]

---

[a] Martin Merzer, *The Miami Herald*, September 7,1990.

Our Search for Prophetic Truth

First, we will once again savor the beautiful Bible prophesies that led to the first coming of Jesus.

We then will examine some of the many Scriptures that give us information concerning His Second Coming and the end of our present world system.

Lastly, we will review the Scriptures used to prove a biblical prohibition concerning "exact dating" of end-time events.

Most of all, as we look at this exciting information, let us thrill together as we view wondrous prophetic pictures painted by God using the brush of Jewish life.

CHAPTER 2
WHERE IS MANKIND HEADED AND WHEN?

Are events in the Middle East leading to some type of Armageddon? If so, does God give any information in the Bible as to when these world-shattering events might occur? Does God tell us when the Rapture and the end of the world will be?

Before we answer these specific questions from a biblical perspective, let's look back at a group of worried men living during the time of Christ on earth. These men, disciples of Jesus, had questions about their futures, much the same as we do. The truth that Jesus would soon be leaving struck panic to their hearts.

Jesus in His usual calm manner comforts His followers by saying, "*Let not your hearts be troubled: ye believe in God, believe also in me. In my Father's house are many mansions: if it were not so I would have told you. I go to prepare a place for you, and if I go to prepare a place for you, I will come again and receive you unto myself; that where I am, there ye may be also. And whither I go ye know and the way ye know.*"

Thomas, who became famous for his habit of verbalizing his doubts, pleads, "*Master, we know not whither thou goest; and how can we know the way?*"

"Jesus saith unto him, I am the way, the truth, and the life, no man cometh unto the Father, but by me."[a]

To understand the full impact of these words on His disciples we must look into the customs of the times. In so doing we will realize the great calming influence these words must have had on His worried followers.

In fact, for nineteen hundred years, millions of readers have been inspired by the words and stories of Jesus written in the four Gospels of the New Testament. Jesus, here in His soothing words to the disciples, had alluded to the marriage customs of the day.

Jewish Weddings

Throughout the New Testament, God uses the analogy of a bride and groom to describe the relationship of Jesus to the church.[b] As a groom pledged love to his bride, so Jesus committed His love to believers, pledged to return for us and promised us an eternity spent with Him.[c]

The people of Jesus' day fully understood the betrothal[d] and marriage customs of which He spoke. However, we in the twentieth century need to look at these ceremonies as they were during the first century, to fully understand the significance of Jesus' teachings. This understanding not only deepens our appreciation of God's love for us, it

---

[a] John 14:1-6

[b] A New Testament term for believers in Jesus Christ. Ephesians 5:23-33.

[c] John 14:1-6; Ephesians 5:23-32; Revelation 19:7-9, 21:9 and 22:17

[d] A pre-marriage agreement similar to engagement.

also gives us added insights to prophetic events and offers comfort in a time of world unrest.

Jewish Weddings First-Century Style

When a Jewish young man wished to marry a particular young woman, it was customary for the prospective groom's father first to approach the girl's father with the proposal of marriage. The two men would discuss this possible union including the price[a] offered by the groom for the bride. If the girl's father agreed to the suggested amount, the two men sealed the agreement with a toast of wine.

The potential bride then entered the room whereupon the prospective groom proclaimed his love and asked her to be his bride. If the young woman wished to be his wife, she accepted his proposal at this time. The validation of the agreement made by the engaged couple was the presentation of a gift by the groom. He offered it in the presence of at least two witnesses. As he gave the gift, usually a ring, he said to his intended bride, "Behold you are consecrated unto me with this ring according to the laws of Moses and Israel."

Arrangements were also made right then concerning the terms of the marriage. A written contract listed the time, place, and size of the wedding as well as recording the dowry and terms of maintenance of the marriage. This binding document called a "ketubah" was kept in the bride's possession until the consummation of the marriage.[15] Finally, this first part of a two-part ceremony

---

[a] The price paid by the groom was called a dowry.

was concluded by the toast of a glass of wine.[16] The whole ceremony was called the "Shiddukhin,"[a] or engagement.

The Bible refers to the status of the prospective bride and groom as "espousal" or "betrothal." It meant that the two people were committed to each other as much as a married couple would be. The only parts of the marriage not yet completed were the formal "huppah" ceremony followed by their physical union. This betrothal was considered so binding that the only way to break it was by an actual bill of divorcement.[17]

The groom then departed, but not before he assured his bride with the promises of building a home for her and returning to complete the marriage ceremony. He usually took a year to prepare her new home which often consisted of an addition built onto his own father's house.[18]

The bride was expected to remain true to her groom as she prepared herself and her trousseau. She lived for the day of his return for her which would be heralded by a shout from the members of the wedding party. The impending return of her groom was to influence the bride's behavior during this interim espousal period.

The typical Jewish wedding took place at night.[19] As soon as any members of the wedding spotted the moving torches signaling the groom's approach, their cry echoed through the streets, "The bridegroom is coming." The *Wycliffe Bible Encyclopedia* tells us, "Mirth and gladness announced their approach to townspeople waiting in houses along the route to the bride's house."[20] Upon hearing the announcement, the excited bride would drop

---

[a] This Jewish word and others, as well as theological terms, are listed for reference in the glossary.

everything in order to slip into her wedding dress and complete her final personal preparations for marriage.

Rather than the groom entering the bride's house, the bride came out to meet him. The two, accompanied by their wedding party, returned together to the groom's home for the marriage ceremony. Following the public ceremony, the newlyweds entered their bridal chamber to be intimate with each other for the first time. After this union, the groom came out and announced to the wedding guests, "Our marriage is consummated."

Upon receiving the glad news, the wedding party began a "festive" seven-day celebration. The celebration lasted seven days only if this was the first marriage of a virgin girl.[21] During this time the bride and the groom stayed with each other in seclusion. At the end of this time of privacy, the groom would present his unveiled bride to everyone in attendance. The newlyweds then joined in the wedding feast with the guests.

Jesus the Groom, Believers the Bride

In the Bible, God describes mankind by such unflattering examples as dumb sheep, foolish builders, temporary grass, vipers, ornate tombs, and blind leaders of the blind. Of course these and other disparaging descriptions fit us all too well. But, because of God's great love, He has other, quite compassionate ways to describe His feelings toward those who respond to His offer of salvation. He gives us such wonderful titles as sons, joint heirs with Christ, beloved, and children. One of the most tender terms used to describe us is "the bride, the Lamb's wife."[a]

---

[a] Revelation 21:9

We just reviewed customs surrounding first-century Jewish betrothals and weddings. Now let's explore how these might relate to us as Christians today. Then let's seek to uncover the possible prophetic information presented in these ceremonies.

In eternity past, God the Father and God the Son planned our salvation.[a] The Bible states concerning God, *"He hath chosen us in him before the foundation of the world."*[b] They settled the price long before the offer of salvation was given to us. We see God the Father as the "father of the groom" and because Jesus is actually the creative person of the Godhead,[c] He stands in as the "the father of the bride."

How encouraging to realize this offer of love was not an afterthought of God. In fact, the Scripture refers to Jesus as *"the lamb slain from the foundation of the world."*[d]

Jesus (in the form of a man) also steps into the role of the prospective groom. He offered **Himself** as the "price" for us, His intended bride. God actually says about us, *"For ye are bought with a price."*[e]

After the plan was established, this loving proposal of salvation was given by Jesus to all mankind. God explains that everyone has the opportunity to respond to His offer. The Bible says, *"For whosoever shall call upon the name of the Lord shall be saved."* *"The heavens declare the glory of God and*

---

[a] Psalm 110:1-4

[b] Ephesians 1:4

[c] Colossians 1:12-18

[d] Revelation 13:8

[e] I Corinthians 6:19, 20

the firmament sheweth his handywork...There is no speech nor language where their voice is not heard." God also warns us that everyone understands who He is, so when people reject this proposal of love they are *"without excuse."*[a]

When we answer "yes" to Jesus' offer of marriage, we become His betrothed. This arrangement is secured by the Holy Spirit, who protects the purchased bride until the return of Jesus. God says, *"Ye were sealed with the Holy Spirit of promise, which is the earnest of our inheritance until the redemption of the purchased possession, unto the praise of his glory."*[b] Our "engagement ring" of promise is none other than the Holy Spirit of God Himself.

Imagine, too, that just as the Jewish bride of long ago held the written promise of marriage commitment (ketubah) in her hand, so the prospective bride of Christ today holds the Bible in her hands. These written promises from Jesus describe His everlasting love and commitment.

On the night before His Crucifixion, Jesus drank a glass of wine with His followers. Lifting the cup He declared, *"This cup is the New Testament in my blood, which is shed for you."* Paul reminds us that Jesus commanded, *"This do ye, as oft as ye drink it, in remembrance of me."*[c] Just as the groom in a Jewish marriage toasted his espoused bride, so we, by the communion cup, remember our betrothal to Jesus and the supreme price He paid for us.

Jesus said He must leave us in order to go back to His Father's house and prepare our new home. He promised

---

[a] Romans 10:13; Psalm 19:1, 3; Romans 1:18-20

[b] Ephesians 1:13, 14

[c] Luke 22:20; I Corinthians 11:25

also to return and gather all those who constitute His bride and transport them to this new home.[a] This parallels exactly the ancient marriage customs!

For nearly two thousand years, Jesus has been in heaven "preparing a place for us." In God's time, Jesus will *"descend from heaven with a shout, with the voice of the archangel, and with the trump of God... We which are alive and remain shall be caught up together with them in the clouds to meet the Lord in the air: so shall we ever be with the Lord."*[b] This catching away, called by many "the Rapture," is pictured in the Jewish marriage custom. The groom comes to the bride's home and brings her back to the wedding ceremony which is held at his father's house. This is the same house where he has also prepared a home for her.

Although we, the bride of Christ, have known for nearly two thousand years that Jesus would return for us, we have only been able to say, "He's coming back—maybe in my lifetime." *"For our conversation is in heaven; from whence we look also for the Savior, the Lord Jesus Christ."*[c]

We have, of necessity, spent a portion of our lives involved in mundane matters since we didn't know the exact time of His return. However, just as the first-century bride reacted excitedly when she heard the shout across town announcing the impending arrival of her groom, so we as the listening bride of Christ should react when we hear the call, ahead of Jesus' arrival, "The bridegroom is coming."

---

[a] John 14:1-3

[b] I Thessalonians 4:16, 17

[c] Philippians 3:20

The wedding celebration of seven days is carried on by the guests while the bride and groom spend this time in seclusion. At the end of the seven days the groom brings his bride out and her veil is removed for the first time, so all the guests can see her beauty.

This is a picture of the seven-year celebration in heaven which occurs simultaneously with the seven-year time of Tribulation transpiring on earth. The culmination of this time is described in the Bible. *"Let us be glad and rejoice, and give honor to him: for the marriage of the Lamb is come, and his wife hath made herself ready. And to her was granted that she should be arrayed in fine linen, clean and white: for the fine linen is the righteousness of the saints. And he saith unto me, Write, Blessed are they which are called unto the marriage supper of the Lamb."*[a]

John Walvoord writes that "the marriage symbolism is beautifully fulfilled in the relationship of Christ to His Church. Revelation 19:6-9 is actually a prophetic hymn anticipating the marriage of the Lamb and His bride after He has begun His reign, and He will not begin His reign on earth until He has conquered the kings of the earth led by Antichrist."[22]

The Jewish wedding, a perfect picture from beginning to end of Jesus' love for believers, should melt our hearts with appreciation. The prophetic picture is quite accurate, bringing us once again to see that God has woven many time clues in the Scriptures for us to discover.

---

[a] Revelation 19:7-9

✡ ✡ ✡ ✡ ✡ ✡

SECTION II
FEAST DAYS

Other prophetic pictures of Jesus exist in Scripture besides this one in the marriage ceremony. Let's not overlook these lesser-known prepictures. By gaining knowledge of the Jewish life and customs that weave through the whole fabric of the Bible, we can discover magnificent portrayals of Jesus in this Hebrew tapestry.

From Genesis to Revelation, God has embroidered pictures of Jesus in Scripture that foretell His original coming as Messiah (called the Incarnation), His snatching away of the believers (known as the Rapture), and His return to reign on earth (called His Second Coming).

A particularly exciting realm of prophecy is found in the Jewish feast days. Throughout history, numerous spiritual events have occurred on these pre-established Jewish Holy days. These events not only occurred on Jewish celebration days, but they also typify the meaning of the celebrations. The timing and message of these fulfillments correspond so well to the earlier celebrations, that Bible students realize the match-ups are not accidental.

These non-coincidental similarities demonstrate the principle of **veiled information being hidden in the Feast days.** Colossians 2:16-17 verifies this concept. *"Let no man therefore judge you in meat or in drink, or of the new moon, or of the sabbath days: <u>Which are a shadow of things to come</u>."* This principle obligates students of the Bible to pursue a deeper understanding of these God-given festivals. Another

Scripture describing the principle of hidden information being typified in Old Testament Jewish ordinances is, *"priests...who serve unto the example and the shadow of heavenly things."*[a]

God gives us a complete list of the seven Jewish feasts in Leviticus, chapter 23. In verse two, God says to Moses, *"Speak unto the children of Israel, and say unto them, Concerning the feasts of the Lord, which ye shall proclaim to be holy convocations, even these are my feasts."*

It is noteworthy, as brought out by Coulson Shepherd in *Jewish Holy Days,*[23] that the meaning of the Hebrew word "mowar" translated "feasts"[b] carries the thought, "to keep an appointment." It also ties in with our study to note the Hebrew word "miqraw" translated "holy convocation," means "a public meeting or a rehearsal."

Perhaps these feasts are pictures of God's appointments with mankind. Could these holy convocations, given to the Jews, actually be rehearsals of future great events on God's calendar?

Using the premise that all of the Old Testament ordinances have a New Testament and/or prophetic importance, let's explore the seven feasts mandated by God to the Jews.

✡   ✡   ✡   ✡   ✡   ✡

---

[a] Hebrews 8: 4,5

[b] Hebrew word "mowed." *Strong's Exhaustive Concordance of the Bible,* Hebrew Lexicon Section, entry #4150, an appointment or fixed time.

The Jewish Calendar

By Jewish months, the seven feasts in Leviticus 23 are:

FEAST	JEWISH MONTH	HEBREW WORD
1. PASSOVER	Nisan 14 (falls in April or May)	Pesach
2. UNLEAVENED BREAD	Nisan 15	Hag-Ha-Matzot
3. FIRSTFRUITS	It begins "on the morrow after the Sabbath"ᵃ following Passover.	Bikkurim
4. FEAST OF WEEKS	It begins fifty days after Firstfruits. (falls in May or June)	Shavuot
5. FEAST OF TRUMPETS	Tishri 1 (September or October)	Rosh HaShanah
6. DAY OF ATONEMENT	Tishri 10	Yom Kippur
7. FEAST OF TABERNACLES	Tishri 15	Succoth

ᵃ Sabbath is the Hebrew word "to stop, or cease from labor." It is the name of the Jewish seventh day of the week which corresponds with the Gentile calendar days of Friday night and Saturday daylight hours. The word Sabbath is also used to describe some special holy days in the Bible.

The God-given dates of these feasts offer enlightenment concerning both the original and prophetic meanings of the feasts. These dates seem confusing at first since the Jewish calendar is uniquely different from all other calendars. This difference comes because the Hebrew calendar is determined by the moon's position, while the Gentile or Gregorian calendar is based on the movement of the sun.

The two different systems cause the Gregorian calendar dates to correspond only generally with the Hebrew calendar dates, thus making exact comparison difficult.

God originally designated Nisan (Abib) as the first month of the Hebrew calendar.[24] This sequence became known as the religious calendar. Later the Jews introduced a civil calendar which instituted the month of Tishri as the first month of the year causing Tishri 1 to become the Jewish "New Year's Day."

Two Ways of Beginning a "Day"

One other important facet of the Jewish calendar system is the distinctive time a new day is started. A new day is declared on the exact moment of sundown (approximately 6:00 P.M.). This system of day counting is based on the creation story as outlined in Genesis chapter 1 which defines each day as "evening and morning." Of course this is in contrast to the Gregorian or Gentile system which begins each new day at 12:00 midnight.

The following chart shows the months of both calendars, the occurrences of the feast days, and how they correspond in the years 1994–1997. Notice the way the feasts occur on different days of the month in the Gregorian versus the Jewish calendar.

The first three feasts are grouped close together in the first month, then the fourth feast is fifty days later. Next, there is a gap of almost four months, and then the last three feasts follow in the seventh month.

CALENDAR YEAR OF FEASTS
(sample as celebrated by Jews today)

LUNAR JEWISH CALENDAR Feasts and Months in Hebrew		SOLAR GREGORIAN CALENDAR Feasts and Months in English				
			1994	1995	1996	1997
Pesach	Nisan 14	Passover	March 27	April 15	April 4	April 22
Hag-Ha-Matzot	Nisan 15	Unleavened Bread	March 28	April 16	April 5,	April 23
Bikkurim	Nisan 16	Firstfruits	March 29	April 17	April 6	April 24
	Iyar					
Shavout	Silvan 50th day after Firstfruits	Feast of Weeks	May 16	June 4	May 24	June 11
	Tamuz					
	Av					
	Elul					
Rosh HaShanah	Tishri 1	Trumpets	September 6	September 26	September 14	October 2
Yom Kippur	Tishri 10	Atonement Day	September 15	October 4	September 23	October 11
Succoth	Tishri 15	Tabernacles	September 20	October 9	September 28	October 16

Everything God does, everything recorded in His Word, is exactly what He wants to convey to mankind. The numbers, the dates, the stories; all have been designed and recorded for His purposes. Jesus, referring to the smallest symbols in Hebrew writing, says, "*One jot or one tittle shall in no wise pass from the law, till all be fulfilled*" (Matthew 5:18).

Let's view the significance of the feast days held for the Jews, then scrutinize the feasts for prophetic importance.

CHAPTER 3
PASSOVER (Feast #1)

SPRING
NISAN 14
Preparation for Passover

The descendants of Abraham, Isaac, and Jacob constitute the nation of Israel. In fact, Jacob's name was changed to Israel by God. God promised all three of these progenitors that their descendants would own the land of Canaan forever. During a severe famine, when this clan numbered only seventy, Pharaoh invited them to move into Egypt. Later, because the Jews multiplied to a respectable-size nation, the Egyptians (fearing an internal take-over) forced the Israelites into slavery.

God warned Pharaoh in Exodus, chapter 4, *"Thus saith the Lord, Israel is my son, even my firstborn: And I say unto thee, Let my son go, that he may serve me: and if thou refuse to let him go, behold, I will slay thy son, even thy firstborn."*[a] Then through nine successive plagues,[25] God continued to ask Pharaoh to release His people to go into the desert on a three-day journey to offer sacrifice unto the Lord.

---

[a] Exodus 4:22-23

Pharaoh acquiesced, agreeing to their release in order to cause the plagues to stop, but then each time he changed his mind and refused to let them go.

Ultimately, God's message came that He would indeed kill the firstborn of every family in Egypt. This last judgment devastated Pharaoh, and finally caused him to release the Jewish slaves for their time of worship.

Amazingly, God had given their revered ancestor Abraham the details of this migration, slavery, and exact time of release.[a]

The feast of Passover commemorates this time in Egypt when the Lord spared the lives of the firstborn Jews. God literally "passed over" the homes of those who had believed and obeyed His instructions for safety.

Through Moses, God had instructed the Jews that on the tenth day of Nisan each household must select a male lamb without blemish. They obeyed God, and after carefully selecting their lambs to insure perfection, they killed them on the fourteenth day of this first month. God also commanded, "*Neither shall ye break a bone thereof.*" They were instructed to "*take of the blood and strike it on the two side posts and on the upper door post of the houses.*" God explained how they must roast the meat and eat it along with unleavened bread and bitter herbs. None of the sacrificed lamb could remain until the morning.[b] He finished the outline of Passover by commanding the Jews to commemorate their release from bondage by celebrating this feast every year at the same time.

---

[a] Genesis 15:13-16

[b] Exodus 12:1-13; Leviticus 23:4, 5

According to Jewish scholars, this passover meal,[a] as outlined in the Torah,[b] was repeated every year on the fourteenth day of Nisan except for the ritual of smearing of the blood on the lintel and side posts which "was never duplicated again."[26]

When the Jews built the Tabernacle and later the Temple, the Passover killing transferred from their homes to God's appointed center of sacrifice.[c] The heads of each family still killed their own lamb, but it was all done inside the Temple court.[27]

The Jewish historian, Josephus, gives an interesting insight concerning the immense number of lambs used for Passover during a first-century celebration. He states, "A company not less than ten belong to every sacrifice (for it is unlawful for them to feast singly by themselves), and many of us are twenty in a company."[28] He calculated that on a first-century Passover 256,500 lambs were slain!

Twelve Fulfillments

The prophetic significance of this holy day of Passover is many-fold. I Corinthians 5:7 explains, *"For even Christ our passover is sacrificed for us."* Also the Apostle John

---

[a] Called Seder in Hebrew.

[b] The Torah is the first five books of the Jewish Bible, also known as "The Law." Torah is sometimes used in a general sense by Jews when referring to their whole (Old Testament) Bible although "Tanakh" is used the most often. Interestingly, the word "Tanakh" is an acronym composed of the first letters of the three sections of the Hebrew Bible, 1) The Law (Torah); 2) the Prophets (Neviim); and 3) the Writings (Khetuvim).

[c] Deuteronomy 16: 1-6

pointing to Jesus declares, "*Behold the <u>Lamb of God</u> which taketh away the sin of the world.*"[a]

Comparing the rituals in Exodus regarding the Passover lamb to the events which transpired before and during the Crucifixion of Jesus brings us to a reverent conclusion that Jesus is indeed the Lamb of God. Let's look at twelve of these fulfillments.

1. **Passover and Crucifixion preplanned by God**: Both the original Passover and its fulfillment in Jesus' Crucifixion were prophesied by God long before they occurred.

Words of promise given by God to Abraham include a prophecy concerning his descendants. God foretold, "*Know of a surety that thy seed shall be a stranger in a land that is not theirs, and shall serve them; and they shall afflict them four hundred years;*

And also that nation, whom they shall serve, I will judge: and afterward shall they come out with great substance."[b]

Just as God foretold, Abraham's descendants all moved to Egypt upon the invitation of a friendly Pharaoh. However, after thirty years, the subsequent Pharaohs began turning against the Jews, eventually forcing them to become slaves. In time, the Jews cried out to God to deliver them from bondage. The Lord answered their cry through Moses whom He had prepared for this task. Exactly 430 years later (**to the day**), the Passover and ensuing exodus occurred.[c] [29]

---

a   John 1:29

b   Genesis 15:13,14

c   Exodus 12:40, 41; Acts 7:6, 7

The birth and Crucifixion of Jesus was also pre-planned by God. Scripture tells us that Mary conceived a child of the Holy Spirit. We also read, "*And she shall bring forth a son, and thou shalt call his name Jesus: for he shall save his people from their sins.*"[a] In fact seven hundred years earlier Isaiah prophesied: "*Behold a virgin shall conceive, and bear a son, and shall call his name Immanuel.*"[b]

Jesus is actually referred to in the Scriptures as "*the lamb slain from the foundation of the world.*"[c] (That's certainly preplanning!)

2. **Choice of city:** The divine plan to provide Jesus as the ultimate Passover lamb is demonstrated in God's choice of Bethlehem as the birth city.

Travelers streaming into Jerusalem for the yearly celebration of Passover needed to purchase lambs for sacrifice. In fact, one particular city had raised lambs for this purpose since Old Testament times. When one visits Israel today, the tour guides often point out this town as "the city where the sacrificial lambs were raised." It is Bethlehem![d] Imagine! Jesus, "*the Lamb of God which taketh away the sin of the world,*" was born in the same city which, for more than one thousand years, had provided sacrificial lambs for Passover.

---

[a] Matthew 1:21

[b] Isaiah 7:14

[c] Revelation 13:8

[d] A comparison of Genesis 35:19-21 to Micah 4:8 and 5:2 by David Hocking (Calvary Chapel, Costa Mesa, CA) in his tape series on Genesis demonstrates clearly that Bethlehem was the place where the Jews raised lambs for sacrifice.

Notice at the time of Jesus' birth, Old Testament scholars were well aware of the prophecy that Messiah would be born in Bethlehem. The Bible says of Herod, after *"he had gathered all the chief priests and the scribes of the people together, he demanded of them where Christ should be born.*

And they said unto him, In Bethlehem of Judea: for it is written by the prophet,

And thou Bethlehem in the land of Judah, art not the least among the princes of Judah: for out of thee shall come a Governor that shall rule my people Israel."[a]

3. **Without blemish:** As the Passover lamb must be a male without blemish, so Jesus was a male without blemish. In I Peter 1:18,19 God makes sure we understand that His Son was *"a lamb without blemish and without spot."* Throughout Jesus' ministry, critics looked for some error, some blemish, to use as a legal reason to reject His claim to be the Son of God, the Messiah.[30] This examination climaxed in an enveloping assault by all of His religious antagonists to find some error in His life or teaching. This unsuccessful attack began after Jesus' triumphal entry into Jerusalem when He offered Himself to the Jews.[b]

4. **Selected on a specific day:** Jesus was dedicated as God's sacrificial lamb on the appropriate prophetic day. Just as fifteen hundred years earlier, the Passover lamb was selected on this tenth day of Nisan, so Jesus was set apart for sacrifice on the same date. This can be determined by following the biblical progression of days

---

[a] Matthew 2:4-6

[b] Matthew 21:1-9; Mark 11:1-11; Luke 19: 29-38; John 12:12-19

listed in John 12:1-12: *"Then Jesus six days before the passover came to Bethany."*

This passage goes on to tell us that Jesus ate dinner that evening in Bethany, was anointed with oil by Mary, then *"on the next day"* He proceeded through His triumphal entry.

According to the *Jewish Encyclopedia,* counting of days can be inclusive. That is, the count of "one" can begin during a portion of the day on which you begin counting. By simply counting, we can discover that the day which is *"six days before the Passover"* is the ninth day of Nisan. (*note following chart*)

HEBREW DAY	GREGORIAN DAY

From sundown to sundown (approx. 6 PM) A day is referred to as "night and day"	From 12 midnight to 12 midnight A day is referred to as "day and night"

That means Jesus traveled and arrived in Bethany on the ninth of Nisan before sundown.[a] As He ate dinner the evening which began Nisan 10, Mary anointed Jesus with costly perfumed oil. This expensive ointment was used primarily for anointing dead bodies because it gave the deceased a sweet smell.[31]

---

[a] Edersheim in *The Life and Times of Jesus the Messiah* pp. 357, 358 (see bibliography) places the arrival of Jesus on Friday and the supper on Sabbath. (Further discussion of this point will follow.)

Judas Iscariot immediately criticized this use of oil as an extravagant expenditure of funds. Jesus answered his objection by saying, *"Let her alone; against this day of my burying hath she kept this."*[a]

The significance of Mary's actions can be discovered in over one hundred references to "anointing" in the Old Testament. A special recipe in Exodus lists the ingredients God wanted in His holy oil. Numerous fragrant spices stirred into olive oil produced the holy oil used for consecrating kings, priests, and objects used in service to the Lord.[b] It was also spread on the unleavened bread that was given as an offering to the Lord.[c]

Jesus actually explained that Mary's anointing consecrated Him to God for a sacrificial death.

5. **Testing:** The time of Jesus' testing was both the **same length of time** and the **exact dates** that the Passover lambs were originally selected and examined to insure perfection, while staked outside each home to await sacrifice!

"The next day" of John 12:12 was[d] the triumphal entry of Jesus.[e] This donkey ride into Jerusalem gave a chance for

---

[a] John 12:7

[b] Exodus 29:7, 30:22-33

[c] Exodus 29:2; I Samuel 15:1; Leviticus 8:10

[d] Since the activities of the triumphal entry as well as the traveling Jesus did by coming to Bethany would have broken the Sabbath rules of work and travel, it appears that Jesus had supper Friday evening at Bethany and received local guests only until the Sabbath day was over. This places the triumphal entry on Sunday, Nisan 11.

[e] Many call this day Palm Sunday.

the Jewish nation to receive their Messiah, God's anointed sacrificial lamb. God's offer to the Jews was prophesied in 487 B.C.: *"Rejoice greatly, O daughter of Zion; shout O daughter of Jerusalem: behold thy King cometh unto thee: he is lowly, and riding upon an ass, and upon a colt the foal of an ass."*[a]

As He rode through the streets that day, it appeared that Jesus would be received as the crowds waved palm branches and sang out, *"Hosanna: Blessed is the King of Israel that cometh in the name of the Lord."*[b] How wonderful! The waving of palms along with these words of praise from the Psalms are all part of the Jewish liturgy welcoming the expected Messiah to His Kingdom.[c] Did these celebrants actually recognize Jesus as the Son of God, their Messiah? Unfortunately, as we trace this adoring crowd, a scant three days later we hear most of these same people shouting, *"Crucify him, crucify him !"*[d]

Also this "triumphal" day was the beginning of an intense period of testing by the religionists, as related in all four Gospels:[e] *"Then went the Pharisees, and took counsel how they might entangle him in his talk."*[f]

After being anointed for burial, the scrutiny by His antagonists lasted four days. Finally, the accusers gave up trying to find fault with Jesus. No error could be found in

---

[a] Zechariah 9:9

[b] John 12:13

[c] *See* chapter on "Feast of Tabernacles," for more concerning this celebration.

[d] Luke 23:21

[e] Matthew 22:15-23:39; Mark 12:13-40; Luke 20:1-47; John 12:20-50

[f] Matthew 22:15

Him. They instead decided to crucify him with the assistance of false witnesses. These false witnesses couldn't even agree in their lies against Him, and Pilate finally pronounced the actual words, *"I find in him no fault at all."*[a]

6. **Blood provided life:** Jesus came to die. Just as the blood of the Passover lamb sprinkled around the doorway saved the lives of the firstborn children in that house, so the blood of Jesus provides life to those who believe in Him and take shelter in His sacrifice.

God's purpose for blood in sacrifice is explained in Leviticus 17:11, *"For the life of the flesh is in the blood: and I have given it to you upon the altar to make an atonement for your souls: for it is the blood that maketh an atonement for the soul."*

Jesus applied this to himself during the Last Supper as He spoke to His disciples[b], *"And He took the cup, and gave thanks, and gave it to them, saying, drink ye all of it: For this is my blood of the New Testament, which is shed for many for the remission of sins."*

Finally, to make the blood significance very clear to us, God's Word says[c], *"How much more shall the blood of Christ, who offered himself without spot to God, purge your conscience from dead works to serve the living God?"*

7. **No bones broken:** Remember, back in Egypt the Jews were expressly instructed not to break any bones of

---

[a] John 18:38

[b] Matthew 26:27, 28

[c] Hebrews 9:14

the Passover lamb. The Roman soldiers customarily broke the leg bones of crucified prisoners in order to hasten death. However the Bible **specifically tells us** that the soldiers did not break the legs of Jesus! *"The Jews therefore, because it was the preparation, that the bodies should not remain upon the cross on the sabbath day, (for that sabbath was an high day), besought Pilate that their legs might be broken, and that they might be taken away. But when they came to Jesus, and saw that he was dead already, **they brake not his legs.**"*[a]

8. **Many lambs represented one person:** Based on the number of Jews who left in the Exodus and each household's need for a sacrifice, the first Passover probably required more than 100,000 lambs.[b] Considering the immense number of lambs sacrificed, take notice of the peculiar way God referred to these lambs in Exodus. God instructed Moses, *"And the whole assembly of the congregation of Israel shall kill it in the evening."*[c]

God's amazing design is revealed when, despite the existence of thousands of sacrificial lambs, He refers to the sacrifices as a singular "it." This again is a prepicture of Jesus, *"the Lamb of God which taketh away the sin of the world."*[d] This specific preview of Jesus is mentioned with excitement by both J. Vernon McGee and Arthur Pink as well as other noted scholars.[32]

---

[a] John 19:31, 33

[b] Exodus 12:37

[c] Exodus 12:6

[d] John 1:29

9. **Crucified on Passover Day:** These comparisons reveal not only that the Passover lamb was a picture of Jesus Christ, they also show us another amazing parallel. He was crucified on **the exact day of Passover!** While the Jews were actually killing the lambs in preparation for the passover celebration,[33] Jesus was being crucified. Matthew 26:2 states, "*Ye know that after two days is the feast of the passover, and the Son of man is betrayed to be crucified.*" John 13:1 tells us, "*Now before the feast of the passover, when Jesus knew that his hour was come that he should depart out of this world unto the Father.*" This is also clearly brought out in John 19:14, 15, "*It was the <u>preparation of the passover,</u> and about the sixth hour; and he saith unto the Jews, Behold your King! But they cried out, Away with him. Pilate saith unto them, Shall I crucify your King? The chief priests answered, We have no king but Caesar.*"

10. **Hung on the cross as sacrificial lambs brought, and died at the exact moment sacrificial killing began:** From instructions in Exodus to "*kill it in the evening*," we learn the time that the original Passover lambs were killed. This term "evening" was an idiom meaning "between evenings" which referred to the time of 3:00 P.M. until 6:00 P.M.[34] We also have other information that confirms this time slot for the slaying of the Passover lambs.

The *Encyclopedia Judaica* states, "It became a general custom to refrain from labor from 12:00 (noon) onward since from that time the Paschal sacrifice could properly be brought."[35]

Records also show us that each year at Passover, the priests made sure "the daily burnt offerings were done early, **half past the seventh hour** (1:30 P.M.)[a] to

---

[a] Emphasis and Gregorian time is mine.

accommodate Paschal[a] offerings.["][36] According to the
Encyclopedia Judaica, the last killing at 1:30 P.M. allowed the
offering of the daily sacrifice to be completed by 2:30 P.M.[37]

Even writers in Judaism see these events as
overlapping. They write, "The Gospel of John...dates the
death of Jesus to the 14th of Nisan to the hour of the
Passover slaughtering."[38]

According to the records of Josephus, the high priests
officiated over the Passover sacrifices from 3:00 P.M. until
5:00 P.M.[39]

When we look yet closer at the events of the
Crucifixion day, an astounding probability emerges!

Matthew, Mark, and Luke all refer to a darkness that
came over all the earth from 12:00 noon **until 3:00** P.M.[b]
Since the use of electricity was yet two thousand years
away, it seems highly unlikely that the killing of the
Passover lambs could have begun until God Himself
turned the lights back on **at 3:00** P.M.!

God gives the exact time of Jesus' death as 3:00 P.M.[c] It
appears that not only was Jesus crucified on Passover, He
actually died for us on the cross at 3:00 P.M., the **exact
moment** that the slaying of the Passover lambs began!

Isn't it overwhelming to see how the seemingly out-of-
control mob who crucified Jesus was, in reality, in the
hand of God's perfect timing?

---

[a] Passover.

[b] Matthew 27:45; Mark 15:33; Luke 23:44, 45

[c] Matthew 27:46-50; Mark 15:34-37; Luke 23:44-46. (Note in these Scriptures the
Jewish time is listed which counted 6:00 A.M. as the first hour.)
How awesome to see also in these references (as well as John 19:30) that even
the specific act of dying was done voluntarily by Jesus!

11. **Not left on cross overnight:** Remember, the Jews were expressly instructed not to leave any of the sacrificed lamb until the next morning.

God painted another picture of Jesus in His guidelines for Passover. Notice, the Jews insisted that His body not stay on the cross overnight. While it appears the Jews' motives were connected with keeping the letter of the law concerning dead bodies,[a] they unknowingly fulfilled the rule of **not keeping any of the sacrifice until the next morning.**

12. **Passover night meant death to some and life to others:** Anyone residing in Egypt during Passover night risked the loss of the firstborn child in their home. It didn't matter if they were brave or scared, rich or poor, kind or stingy, religious or atheistic, they all were subject to God's judgment. Only one trait saved their children's lives. That trait was faith—faith that prompted them to follow God's instructions to place the lamb's blood above and beside their doorway.

While the death in each unbelieving home is tragic, the description of the salvation of children in the believing homes is awesome: *"For the Lord will pass through to smite the Egyptians; and when He seeth the blood upon the lintel and upon the two side posts, the Lord will pass over the door, and will not suffer the Destroyer to come in unto your houses to smite you."*[b]

Arthur Pink gives this heartwarming comment in *Gleanings From Exodus,* "It was not merely that the Lord

---

[a] Deuteronomy 21:22, 23

[b] Exodus 12:23

passed by the houses of the Israelites, but that He stood on guard *protecting* each blood-sprinkled door!"[40]

An Unanswered Question

Jewish scholars have puzzled over the meaning of the rules attached to this feast. I'd like to quote and then comment on this astounding statement **from one of their writers.**

"In particular the Chinuch (no. 7)[a] suggests that the emancipation of the Jewish slaves converted them into a 'priestly kingdom.' The 'pesach'[b] was therefore served as a royal feast, and it was to be eaten in the manner of royalty. Consequently, the meat was to be well roasted, a process preferred by royalty because the taste of the meat is brought out to best advantage. Similarly, no bones were to be broken because royalty discards the bones whole, but the poor break the bones so that they can pick them bare of their meat. This homiletic interpretation is not consistent with the provision for the eating of the lamb with matzah and bitter herbs, in commemoration of affliction and bitterness. **One could hardly commemorate royalty and poverty at the same time.**"[41c]

In short, this Jewish theologian is puzzling over the presence of both royalty and affliction in the typology of the Passover meal. He believes the remembrance of royalty and the remembrance of poverty at the same time is incompatible.

---

[a] Jewish commentary

[b] Passover.

[c] Emphasis mine.

This portion of the Passover table has indeed been a stumbling block to the Jews, as predicted by **their own King David.** David writes, "*Let their table become a snare before them: and that which should have been for their welfare, let it become a trap.*"[a]

Christians see no conflict in one feast that celebrates both affliction and royalty. This portion of the feast is seen as a God-designed picture of Jesus Christ as the suffering Savior and the future reigning King.

After the time of King David, upon finishing the Passover meal, those gathered around the Passover table sang the Hallel (Psalms 113–118).[b] Woven into these psalms is another solemn warning from God. He speaks, even in the songs sung at Passover, concerning the expected refusal of the Jews to recognize the Savior Jesus, the Lamb of the Passover: "*The stone which the builder refused is become the headstone of the corner.*"[c] We know this is a reference to Jesus from the Scripture. "*Behold, I lay in Sion a chief corner stone, elect, precious: and he that believeth on him shall not be confounded.*

Unto you therefore which believe he is precious: but unto them which be disobedient, the stone which the builders disallowed, the same is made the head of the corner.

And a stone of stumbling, and a rock of offence, even to them which stumble at the word, being disobedient: whereunto also they were appointed."[d]

---

[a] Psalm 69:22

[b] This is the hymn referred to in Mark 14:22-26.

[c] Psalm 118:22

[d] I Peter 2:6-8

Let us who claim the name of Christ, beware lest we also disregard the deep, personal significance represented in Passover. For our sakes Jesus *"became poor,"* that through His poverty we might be rich,[a] was *"afflicted for our sin,"*[b] and is also our *"King of Kings."*[c] Yes, we know that as King, He will reign on earth during the future Millennium, but He should also be reigning in our hearts today.[d] As Jesus enjoined, *"Why call ye me, Lord, Lord, and do not the things I say?"*[e]

One More Picture

Discovering that the Passover Lamb differs from all other sacrifices unveils a poignant picture of God's great love for us. Rabbi Bloch reveals this difference by drawing attention to the original Hebrew word used to describe the Passover Lamb. He points out that this word is different than the Hebrew word used to describe other biblical sacrifices. He writes, "The Bible never labeled the paschal lamb a *karban*. In reply to a child's request for a definition of the lamb, the Bible orders us to tell him it is a *zevech*, a slaughtered animal (Exodus 12:27)."[42] Bloch points out that *zevech* is in contrast to the designation of *karban*, which is the term used in the Bible for other offerings such as burnt offerings, meal offerings, and peace offerings.

---

[a] II Corinthians 8:9

[b] Isaiah 53:5-7; I Peter 2:23, 24

[c] I Timothy 6:14, 15

[d] Revelation 19:16, 20:6; Romans 10:9

[e] Luke 6:46

Compare Bloch's information to God's unique identification of the Passover Lamb. Note God's claim of *"my sacrifice"* and *"the Lord's passover."*[a] God does not declare possession of other sacrifices. Now the love picture becomes quite clear. God established this Passover Lamb as **His** sacrifice. This lamb represents God's provision of a sacrifice for us just as He provided one for Abraham. Remember, Abraham had assured Isaac, *"My son, God will provide himself a lamb for a burnt offering."*[b]

One very touching aspect of the atoning work of Jesus is that He, as God in the flesh, willingly offered himself on the cross to pay for our sins. Jesus forewarned His disciples about His intention to go to the cross. *"He said unto his disciples, Ye know that after two days is the feast of the passover, and the Son of man is betrayed to be crucified."*[c] Again, after His resurrection, Jesus explained this truth to some still confused disciples. *"O fools, and slow of heart to believe all that the prophets have spoken:* **Ought not Christ to have suffered these things,** *and to enter into his glory? And beginning at Moses and all the prophets, he expounded unto them in all the scriptures the things concerning himself."*[d]

Throughout this examination of Passover one marvels at God's control over His sacrifice. We see His control, not only in His dominion over the affairs of men but also over the schemes of Satan.

---

[a] Exodus 34:25, 12:27

[b] Genesis 22:8

[c] Matthew 26:1,2

[d] Luke 24:25-27

Scripture reveals that the night before the Crucifixion, the Devil prompted Judas to betray Jesus.[a] Imagine! Satan truly thought he had planned the ultimate coup against the rulership of God. Even though Satan possesses great intelligence and great power, he lacks spiritual insight. He missed entirely the symbolism of the sacrifices. He had no comprehension of the Old Testament prophesies concerning Christ nor did he remotely envision that after the Crucifixion, Jesus would conquer death.

The Bible states, *"The fear of the Lord is the beginning of knowledge."*[b] Satan had no fear of God so he did not understand Passover. He lacked the capacity to understand the redemptive plan of God. Satan's evil scheme to eliminate Jesus actually fulfilled God's prophetic Word.[c]

REVIEW OF FEAST OF PASSOVER (PESACH)

Almost fifteen hundred years before Christ, God called Moses to lead the Jewish nation out of bondage in Egypt. Their release came after the firstborn child in every house of Egypt died at the hand of the Lord. Miraculously, the firstborn in each Jewish family lived because of the lamb's blood they placed around the doorway. The yearly Passover meal is a memorial of those saved lives and the nation's release from slavery.

God's prophetic picture in Passover is His Lamb. Jesus Christ provided salvation and release from bondage for all

---

[a] John 13:2

[b] Proverbs 1:7

[c] Psalm 22; 41:9; Isaiah 53

who trust in the power of His blood and, by faith, place it over the door of their own life.

The **precise** description and instructions of Passover are graphically demonstrated in the Crucifixion of Jesus Christ:

1) Jesus came as foretold. Passover also occurred as foretold!

2) Jesus was born in the city where the Passover lambs were raised!

3) Jesus was a male without blemish just as the lambs were!

4) Jesus was chosen for sacrificial death on the same date that Passover lambs were selected!

5) Jesus was tested for perfection for the same length of time and on the exact dates the Passover lambs were observed!

6) Jesus provided salvation through His blood just as the blood of the Passover lambs provided life!

7) Jesus had no bones broken and neither did the lambs!

8) Jesus was the "one" referred to by God as "it" even though the number of lambs slain was plural!

9) Jesus was crucified on the exact day of Passover!

10) Jesus was crucified not only at the same general time of day as the Passover lambs, apparently He died at the exact moment the first group of Passover lambs were slain!

11) Jesus' body did not remain on the cross overnight just as none of the lamb could remain until morning!

12) Jesus provides life to those who trust Him as God's sacrifice just as life came to Jews who believed God and stayed in the houses marked by the lamb's blood!

CHAPTER 4
UNLEAVENED BREAD (Feast #2)

SPRING	
NISAN 14	NISAN 15
Preparation for Passover	Unleavened Dinner

The celebration of Unleavened Bread began on the Passover preparation day of Nisan 14. To prepare, each family removed all leaven[a] from their homes. This was, and still is, done in obedience to God's command, *"Ye shall put away leaven out of your houses."*[b] Since Jews scrupulously eliminated all leaven from their homes, the only bread eaten during this protracted feast was flat, unleavened bread called matzah. Celebrants ate the Feast of Passover and Unleavened Bread after sundown (which had then become the next day, the 15th of the month). The festival continued for seven days and no work could be done on the first or the last day of the seven.

The observance of this holy convocation commemorated the hurried release of the Jews from

---

[a] More commonly known as yeast. Even without yeast, the natural decay of grain, if it becomes wet, can cause rising to take place. Also, bread dough must be prepared quickly and put in the oven immediately to bake in order to avoid natural rising.

[b] Exodus 12:15

bondage in Egypt; God commanded the Jews to keep this feast as a memorial forever.[a]

The seriousness of putting away the leaven is demonstrated by God's penalty against anyone who disobeyed His command. He said if anyone failed to remove leaven, not only from their bread and their homes but even from their territory, "*That soul shall be cut off from Israel.*"[b]

Throughout the centuries, observant Jews have demonstrated extreme dedication in erasing all traces of leaven from their homes and baking areas during this feast. Early in history, bakers prepared matzah with designs or figures but this practice ultimately was forbidden by the rabbis. They feared that if too much time passed in the preparation of an intricate design, some natural rising might occur in the bread, thus breaking the law. Forms or molds to stamp figures on the dough were also prohibited because, the rabbis reasoned, a little piece of dough might get caught in the mold and might not be noticed and that little piece might rise!

Eventually, the only design that appeared on each matzah was one of perforations. These holes were produced by bakers using a sharp-toothed wheel called a *redel*, which they rolled across the dough to prevent rising during baking. Pressing lines on the matzah produces "striping" which also slows down the natural rising process and causes the matzah to be more brittle.

---

[a] Exodus 12:14-20; Leviticus 23:6-8

[b] Exodus 12:15, 19, 13:7; Deuteronomy 16:4

One Jewish writer beautifully captures the important symbolism of the unleavened bread. "These matzot[a] commemorated the speed and the abruptness with which the Jews had to leave Egypt, testifying to the decisive intervention of the Almighty, which compelled Pharaoh to suddenly release the Jews in spite of his relentless opposition. The matzot were thus symbolic of redemption."[b43]

The Spiritual Meaning Of Leaven

Bread baked without leaven is plain and flat but **does not spoil.** The presence of leaven in dough causes bread to rise and become full but, in time, this fluffy bread will mold and become inedible. This occurs because leaven is actually a live fungus!

We are taught in the Bible that leaven is a picture of sin and false religion. Sin, like the expansion that leaven produces, may appear attractive but it promotes decay. Note Jesus' statements, *"Take heed and beware of the leaven of the Pharisees and of the Sadducees,"*[c] and *"Beware ye of the leaven of the Pharisees, which is hypocrisy."*[d] God cautions us, *"Your glorying is not good. Know ye not that a little leaven leaveneth the whole lump? Purge out therefore the old leaven, that ye may be a new lump, as ye are unleavened. For even*

---

[a] Matzot is plural of matzah.

[b] The overview of Passover is certainly symbolic of redemption as verified in the Song of Moses, Exodus 15:13. *"Thou in thy mercy hast led forth the people which thou hast redeemed."* However, the **specific role** of the bread represents the sanctifying work of Jesus and the goal of sanctification in the life of a believer.

[c] Matthew 16:6

[d] Luke 12:1

Christ our passover is sacrificed for us: Therefore let us keep the feast, not with old leaven, neither with the leaven of malice and wickedness; but with the unleavened bread of sincerity and truth."[a]

What a beautiful picture! Jesus, through His sacrifice, purged sin from mankind. The Bible says, "*How much more shall the blood of Christ, who through the eternal Spirit offered himself without spot to God, purge your conscience?*" and "*without shedding of blood is no remission.*"[b]

Also, this feast prepictures Jesus in the unleavened bread itself. Mary's act of anointing Jesus with fragrant spikenard oil four days before His Crucifixion, reminds us of the scriptural mandate to spread oil on the unleavened bread used for sacrifice.[c] Only Jesus could be represented by unleavened bread because only He lived a sinless life.

Even the preparation of the bread as dictated by the rabbis reminds us of the body of Jesus. Look at a piece of matzah. To be Kosher, it must be striped and pierced. God prophesied concerning the Messiah that, "*With his stripes we are healed.*"[d] Even more startling is God's prophecy that one day yet to come, "*I will pour upon the house of David, and upon the inhabitants of Jerusalem, the spirit of grace and of supplications: and they shall look upon me whom they have pierced, and they shall mourn for him, as one mourneth for his only son.*"[e] Jesus, even in His resurrection

---

[a] I Corinthians 5:6-8

[b] Hebrews 9:14, 22

[c] Numbers 6:15; John 12:1-8

[d] Isaiah 53:5

[e] Zechariah 12:10

body, kept the marks of His Crucifixion. Prophetic
Scripture poignantly describes the holes in His hands and
His sides as eternal testimony to His act of redemptive
love. *"What are these wounds in thine hands? Then he shall
answer, Those with which I was wounded in the house of my
friends."*[a]

Literal, Hidden Truth

Every year at the Passover dinner, a ceremony called
"Seder" takes place. On the original Passover table only
three food items were mandated by God: the lamb which
symbolized redemption, the unleavened bread which
pictured sanctification, and bitter herbs that reminded the
celebrants of their bitterness of affliction as slaves in Egypt
under Pharaoh.

Little remains of God's original Passover table at
present day Seders. We see today's Passover table covered
with a white cloth, on which is placed a large platter called
"ke'arah," containing unique food. This platter holds a
roasted egg, a roasted lamb shankbone, bitter herbs, a
green vegetable, *"haroset"* (a sweet pap mixture), and salt
water. We also see wine cups for each participant and an
extra cup of wine for Elijah.

The only item on the table (besides the bitter herbs)
remaining from the original ones mandated by God in
Exodus is the unleavened bread. An amazing, involved
ceremony connected with this unleavened bread dates
back more than 1900 years. It becomes most intriguing
indeed to discover that Jewish scholars seem vague about
the origin of this matzot-bread ceremony. Some conjecture
that it was originally designed to keep the young children

---

[a] Zechariah 13:6

interested in the Passover ceremony. Perhaps we can discover the literal, hidden meaning in the matzot.

First, we will enter the home of a large family of observant Jews as they close the service by saying, "Next year in Jerusalem." Now, let's listen to a firsthand report of the ceremony as seen through the eyes of a young boy...

"You know, I don't totally understand about the meal we just did, but I can tell you my favorite part! It's the part in the middle when my father takes the three pieces of bread, you know, the matzot that are in the pretty cloth holder. Well, of course each piece of bread is already in its special little compartment you know, the bag's divided. Okay, so he takes out the middle one. (He calls it the *Afikomen*, but it's really just the middle piece of bread.) So then, he breaks it in half, and he wraps one piece in a napkin and then (this is the best part), he hides it under his pillow, 'cause we're all sitting down lying against pillows. (My father says we do that because a long time ago our very old relatives got rescued from Egypt. That's kind of what this Seder's about, you know. They were slaves and had to stand up to eat while everybody else got to sit down and lie on pillows and now because my relatives got rescued and we're not slaves any more, we get to lie on pillows and eat this dinner.)

"Well anyway, the good part comes after everybody drinks their third cup of wine. All of us kids get to hunt for the matzah that my father hid. Whoever finds it gets a great prize after dinner. This year I found it! Of course, I had to bring the bread to my father first so everybody could have a bite of it. (We're required to eat it, you know.)

"I could hardly wait until everybody finished dinner and sang, and of course, my father had to talk some more. He reads Bible words and poems and famous sayings out of the Haggadah.ᵃ (Everything we did tonight is in that book, even the answers to the questions I was supposed to ask my father.) I suppose when I'm older, this whole thing will mean more to me, I mean when I understand what that matzot bread and wine and stuff is all about. Well, anyway, I got my prize...."

Now that we've seen this ancient ceremony through this boy's eyes, let's look for the hidden, literal meaning found in the ceremony of the Afikomen. One amazing fact will emerge. We will discover that even though this ceremony of the Afikomen developed through Jewish tradition and was not mandated by God, its origins are Christian!

Apparently, the practice of this intricate custom dates back to the middle of the first century A.D. How interesting. More specifically, this time period was sometime after A.D. 30 (after Jesus Christ) but before A.D. 70 (the fall of the Temple).

A sharp dividing line between Christians and Jews has existed for 1900 years. This difference in understanding (largely relating to beliefs about Jesus and methods of worship) did not exist until the latter part of the first century A.D. Interestingly, throughout the New Testament, we see numbers of occasions when Jesus reasoned with observant Jews and actually taught in the

---

ᵃ A word that means "narration" or "the telling". It is a guidebook with the whole order of Seder service developed mostly in the first and second century A.D. Centuries later, leading biblical exegetes such as Nahmanides and Maimonides continued to define and refine the order of service.

synagogues. Even though the animosity of some Jews
toward the Hebrew converts caused persecution and
executions, many synagogues welcomed Hebrew
Christians[a] as late as A.D. 60. The Apostle Paul, a leading
Pharisee of the first century, at one time fiercely opposed
adherents of "this way,"[b] but surprisingly (after
recognizing that Jesus was indeed his Messiah) it is
recorded that as late as A.D. 52 that Paul was welcomed in
the synagogue at Ephesus where he spoke *"boldly for the
space of three months, disputing and persuading the things
concerning the kingdom of God."*[c]

One Jewish scholar points out, "The destruction of the
Temple in the year 70 crushed the morale of the Jewish
people and brought a serious crisis to their religious life.
Many must have wondered whether the great misfortune
was a signal of God's rejection of His people." This writer
points out, "The end of the sacrificial offerings left the
festivals without meaning or significance. The popular
Passover night celebration needed considerable
readjustment in order to survive."[44]

Before any Hebrews believed in Jesus Christ as
Messiah, they regularly kept the Feast of Passover and
Unleavened Bread. After recognizing Jesus as the one
pictured in these feasts, the significance of the words He
spoke at the dinner before His Crucifixion became quite
clear to them. The Bible records, *"The Lord Jesus the same*

---

[a] First century Judaism included divisions (similar to denominations) such as
Pharisees, Sadducees, Hellenists, and Essenes. During the middle of the first century,
the Hebrew Christians called "Nazarenes" by some were considered just another sect
within Judaism.

[b] The referral to followers of "this way" was an early version of the designation "The
Way" which became another term for early Christians.

[c] Acts 19:8

night in which he was betrayed took bread: And when he had given thanks, he brake it, and said, Take, eat: this is my body, which is broken for you: this do in remembrance of me."[a] The disciples realized that the bread represented Jesus' body and they obeyed Him by continuing to remember His death, burial and resurrection in the very manner He had instructed them.

Now the relevance of the three pieces of unleavened bread becomes clear. Note, they are placed together in one cloth bag, yet separated from each other by dividers. Early Hebrew Christians recognized the body of Christ in the Unleavened Bread so they designed a beautiful reminder of Him that later become woven into the ceremony of Seder. The three pieces of matzah represent God the Father, God the Son (in the middle compartment) and God the Holy Spirit. See how this ceremony involving the middle piece paints a master portrait of Jesus. The middle piece, the Afikomen, representing Jesus is:

1) taken out of the bag (Jesus came to earth as a man),
2) broken (Jesus died on the cross),
3) wrapped in a cloth (Jesus' body was wrapped in a linen shroud), and
4) hidden under a pillow (Jesus' body was buried in the tomb).
5) Later, after everyone finished their third cup of wine,[b] the children searched the pillows for the hidden piece (Jesus raised again the third day),

---

[a] I Corinthians 11:23, 24

[b] Jewish writers ascribe several names to this third cup including "Cup of Redemption" and "Cup of Blessing."

6) and the child who found the hidden Afikomen received a reward (finding Jesus is the greatest reward possible).

Stunning, momentous information ties this continuing Seder observance to the ceremony of mid-first-century Hebrew Christians. The truth is revealed in the very name of the broken piece of matzah. The word, Afikomen, **is the only Greek word** in the entire Seder ceremony. Why do we find one Greek word in an entirely Hebrew ceremony? Its definition tells the story. This Greek word means, "I came."[a] Imagine! The ceremony of every Passover contains the quiet reminder that Messiah has already come. God once again remains true to His Word. He said His message would always be proclaimed to the world; He even foretold that one day His message would be delivered by nations other than the Jews.[b]

Also note, it was (and still is) mandatory for all persons attending a Seder to eat a piece of the Afikomen. Jesus used the analogy of bread being broken and eaten to teach the disciples that He would be sacrificed to provide salvation for them. He said, "*The bread of God is he which cometh down from heaven, and giveth life unto the world. I am the bread of life: he that cometh to me shall never hunger.*"[c] In a poignant moment, just before His Crucifixion, Jesus reminded His disciples of this truth. "*He took bread, and gave thanks, and brake it, and gave unto them, saying, This is*

---

[a] Jewish writers have varied explanations on how this Greek word came into the Seder. Also their definitions of this Greek word are assorted and vague.

[b] Deuteronomy 32:15-21; Hosea 2:23; Romans 10:13-21

[c] John 6:33, 35

my body which is given for you: this do in remembrance of me."[a]
By the giving of bread to each disciple and by the
necessity in Seder for each celebrant to eat a piece, we see
pictured the fact that on an individual basis, people must
place their faith in the risen Christ.

In addition, the Afikomen must be eaten by midnight,[45]
just as God had commanded earlier that the Passover lamb
must be eaten by midnight.

Overwhelming evidence leads us to conclude that after
the loss of the Temple the newly designed Seder drew
much of its ceremony from the early Hebrew
Christians—ceremonies that Christians had designed to be
a tribute to Jesus Christ, the Messiah.

Even the added custom of providing a cup for Elijah,
along with an empty chair situated in the place of honor at
the table brings us a prepicture of Jesus. The custom
regarding Elijah's cup developed after the fall of the
Temple during the first few centuries A.D. After the loss
of the Temple, God's message still remained in the
Passover dinner.

The Elijah's-cup ritual originated in order to settle a
dispute about the correct number of cups of wine to drink
during the Seder (four or five). Rabbis decreed that a fifth
cup of wine would be poured only for Elijah. They based
this decision on the biblical statement, "*Behold, I will send
you Elijah the prophet before the coming of the great and dreadful
day of the Lord.*"[b] Judaism applies this verse to the belief
that the coming of Elijah must precede the coming of
Messiah. They, in fact, believe that Elijah's coming will be
right at the end of Passover service someday. Based on

---

[a] Luke 22:19

[b] Malachi 4:5

this belief, the youngest son goes outside the house at the end of every Seder to see if Elijah is coming. If the boy returns, telling the expectant celebrants that he cannot see the prophet, then the closing ceremonies of Seder commence. Because of the belief that another whole year must now go by before Elijah can come, the closing words of Seder echo through the air, "Next year in Jerusalem."

How interesting that even the customs added to this feast reflect the expectation for the arrival of Messiah who Christians recognize to be Jesus.

Two More Secrets

Two more vital truths can be deduced from Jewish exposition of the requirements concerning the eating of unleavened bread. To discover these truths, let's first look at the Jews' belief. They teach, "The injunction to eat matzah was obligatory only on the first night, at the paschal feast. There is no obligation, however, to eat matzah during the seven days of the festival of matzot."[46] A careful reading of Scriptures dealing with unleavened bread appears to justify this observation. The Lord required everyone at the Passover dinner to eat some unleavened bread; God also warned that any bread eaten during the other days (of the protracted seven-day feast) must not contain any leaven.

The two spiritual truths gleaned from this information are: 1) The purging, or taking away, of sin that Jesus accomplished on the cross is a vital part of redemption (called sanctification), hence the mandatory eating of the unleavened bread at the Passover dinner (which in its entirety pictured redemption), and 2) the warning to refrain from eating any bread containing leaven during the extended celebration of one week warns every follower of God to choose to avoid sin. This is deduced from God's rule that the eating of matzah was optional during this time. Choosing matzah and abstaining from eating leavened bread depicts the on-going personal responsibility of every believer to abstain from sin. This process is called personal sanctification.

This principle of two strata of sanctification is delineated in *The New Bible Dictionary*. "Christ by His sacrifice sanctifies His brethren. This sanctification, however, is not conceived of primarily as a process but as an accomplished fact, for *'by one offering he hath perfected for ever them that are sanctified'*."[a] This editor goes on to say, "The second meaning of sanctification...concerns the moral and spiritual transformation of the justified believer." In summary the writer states, "There is a progression of moral accomplishment but there is also a mysterious, sanctifying work within him."[47]

We see this second stratum of our responsibility for godly living described as sanctification several times in the Bible. *"For this is the will of God, even your sanctification, that ye should abstain from fornication: that every one of you should know how to possess his vessel in sanctification and honour."* *"And every man that hath this hope in him purifieth himself, even as he is pure."*[b]

Thus we see that God's guidelines (both mandatory and optional eating of unleavened bread) demonstrate the imperative nature of eternal sanctification by the purging work of Christ as well as the believer's responsibility of daily confession and godly living.

---

[a] Hebrews 10:14 (see also Hebrews 10:10)

[b] I Thessalonians 4:3, 4; I John 3:3

REVIEW OF FEAST OF UNLEAVENED
BREAD (HAG-HA MATZOT)

During Passover, the Jews began a week-long celebration which commemorated their hasty departure from Egypt. The only bread eaten during this feast week was unleavened.

Leaven in the Bible is a symbol of sin. This taking away of leaven from the bread is a graphic picture of Jesus' taking away of our sin. Throughout the Feast of Unleavened Bread, the matzah and the ceremonies reveal the sanctifying work of Christ.

How amazing! After Jesus died on the cross, the Jews were commemorating the Feast of Unleavened Bread **at the same time** Jesus was actually purging sin for us!

CHAPTER 5
FIRSTFRUITS (Feast #3)

SPRING		
NISAN 14	NISAN 15	SUN. AFTER SABBATH
Preparation for Passover	Unleavened Dinner	Firstfruits, Resurrection

God instructed Moses in Leviticus 23:10, 11, "*When ye come into the land which I give unto you, and shall reap the harvest thereof, then ye shall bring a sheaf of the firstfruits of your harvest unto the priest: And he shall wave the sheaf before the Lord, to be accepted for you: on the morrow after the sabbath the priest shall wave it.*"

The Jews were to begin celebration of this feast when they arrived in the Promised Land. Leviticus, chapter 23 shows that God gave this ordinance to the Jews so they would remember the first harvest that He would provide for them in the land of Israel.

Israel was instructed to have the high priest bring one sheaf of the firstfruits of the harvest (which represented the whole harvest), and wave it before the Lord. This spring festival became the first harvest celebration of each year.

There is a difference of opinion among theologians, both Jewish and Christian, as to when this feast is to be celebrated. We will take time to examine both viewpoints celebrated. We will take time to examine both viewpoints because of the prophetic application of Firstfruits. A few days difference may seem inconsequential to us, but when God is painting a picture of His beloved Son Jesus Christ, every stroke of His brush is purposeful.

The extreme importance of determining the exact day God intended for the celebration of Firstfruits has to do with the character of God. If He cannot lie, if He is all-knowing, and if nothing is too hard for Him, then the prophetic pictures He paints throughout the Bible must be fulfilled in exact detail!

For instance, if God's Old Testament pictures of Jesus showed us that Jesus would literally be in the grave three days and three nights, then resurrection short of this time period would indicate a lack of knowledge and control on the part of God. As we examine the prophetic pictures of the exact day of both the Crucifixion and the Resurrection, bear in mind the reason for this detailed inspection. God is sovereign! His absolute control over the affairs of man is graphically demonstrated through the timing of the Crucifixion, death, burial, and Resurrection of His beloved Son Jesus Christ.

Different Ideas on Firstfruits

Some commentators have postulated that the Sabbath referred to in Leviticus 23:11 is the Sabbath (Feast) of Unleavened Bread. They conclude that Firstfruits is always to be observed on Nisan 16. It is said by some that a statement of Josephus "proves beyond a doubt" that the Jews celebrated Firstfruits on Nisan 16.[48]

There are several problems with this position. First, it's somewhat precarious to come to a "positive" biblical conclusion based solely on the words of an historian.

Although historical writings are useful in understanding the holy Scriptures, man's words cannot be deemed "inspired."

Historically speaking, the question as to which day or date was the correct one to celebrate Firstfruits has been debated by the Jews themselves. The Pharisees interpreted the Sabbath in Leviticus 23:10-16 to be the Sabbath Feast of Unleavened Bread. This resulted in their celebrating Nisan 16 as Firstfruits which indeed became the predominant view.

We cannot, however, fail to notice that the Sadducees firmly held to their belief that the Sabbath referred to in Leviticus 23 was the seventh-day Sabbath. This system produces a different date each year for the celebration of Firstfruits.

The Qumran community had yet another idea for the celebration of Firstfruits. They used a fixed solar calendar and maintained that the Sabbath at the end of the Passover festival was the one referred to in Leviticus. From this interpretation, Nisan 26 was always celebrated as Firstfruits.[49]

Since the Jews themselves did not agree on the time for Firstfruits and since Jesus made no comment in the Gospels about the feast, we must look beyond tradition to find a solid answer.

With regard to Firstfruits in particular, the scriptural context helps us to determine an understanding of which Sabbath is involved. We can see in Leviticus 23 that five of the seven feasts have definite months and days on which they are to be celebrated.

Note that **no specific date** (i.e., month and day) is given for the Feast of Firstfruits or the Feast of Weeks. Both of these festivals are said to **follow a particular day of the week** by a set number of days. This leads us to see that the day of the month on which they both would fall is variable. They do, however, occur each year on the same day of the week.

This leads us to prefer the selection of Firstfruits as **the Sunday after the Sabbath following Passover.**[a] This interpretation seems more likely, since God left the notable absence of a specific date for this feast.

What Firstfruits Means

The picture presented to us in Firstfruits as New Testament Christians is awe-inspiring! *"But now is Christ risen from the dead, and become the <u>firstfruits</u> of them that slept."*[b] Jesus is the firstfruits from the dead!

Another aspect of this feast can be discovered by reviewing two important pieces of information. From these we will see the careful planning and absolute control of God with regard to Firstfruits and **the year** in which Jesus was crucified.

1. Jesus said He would be at least three days and three nights in the heart of the earth but no longer than three.[c]

2. Easter, when we celebrate **the discovery of the Resurrection** of Jesus, is on Sunday. This allows the three days and three nights to fall between the Crucifixion and Sunday.

---

[a] Danny Litvin in "Pentecost Is Jewish" pp. 3, 9 and Appendix I (see Bibliography) also concurs with this conclusion in his work on this subject.

[b] I Corinthians 15:20

[c] Matthew 27:62-64

According to the original Jewish calendar, every year there would be a different length of time between Passover and Firstfruits. **The year Jesus was crucified,** Passover preceded Sunday by the exact number of days needed to allow **three days** to fit in between. Jesus was crucified on Nisan 14. He conquered death after three days and nights (Nisan 17) so that Sunday the Festival of Firstfruits, on Nisan 18, would be our day to celebrate His Resurrection.

Again, God is altogether true to His Old Testament pictures. As the Jews were following the rituals of Firstfruits, the disciples celebrated the Resurrection of Jesus **in the presence of Jesus,** the firstfruits from the dead!

Prepictured Timing of the Resurrection

The Jews left Egypt on Nisan 15.[a] Through Moses, the Jews had only requested permission to take a three-day journey into the desert to worship the Lord. The Bible states they camped on the shores of the Red Sea which would be the third day or Nisan 17.

Pharaoh once again changed his mind about letting the Jews go to worship the Lord. He mustered his army and galloped into the desert to bring back his Jewish slaves. God surprised everyone by miraculously dividing the waters of the Red Sea, providing a way of escape for the Jews. Pharaoh and his army saw this avenue of escape but when they tried to follow the path prepared through the sea, the water closed over them, drowning everyone.[b]

---

[a] Exodus 12:30, 31

[b] Exodus 14

The count of days involved here has startling significance. Three days from the first Passover, the Jews were delivered from death unto life! The day of Nisan 18 brought jubilation to the rescued Jews. God literally brought them from death unto life.

On that day (Nisan 18) the newly rescued Jews sang, *"Thou in thy mercy hast led forth the people which thou hast redeemed; thou hast guided them in thy strength unto thy holy habitation"*[a] in celebration of their new life. Just so, believers in Jesus Christ now sing, "Because He lives, I can face tomorrow!" The celebration words of the New Testament quoted from the Old Testament prophet Hosea[b] say, *"O death, where is thy sting? O grave, where is thy victory?"*[c]

The amazing rescue of the Jews from the tyrant of Egypt paints a prophetic picture of God's preplanned rescue of all mankind from the ownership of Satan. The Bible says, *"For to this end Christ both died, and rose, and revived, that he might be the Lord of both the dead and the living."*[d] God provided an avenue of life through the Red Sea for the believing Jews, yet this same avenue became a place of judgment for the God-rejecting Egyptians!

This path of either rescue or judgment is still an option to mankind today. The Bible says, *"For God sent not his son into the world to condemn the world; but that the world through him might be saved. He that believeth on him is not condemned:*

---

[a] Exodus 15:13

[b] Hosea 13:14

[c] I Corinthians 15:55

[d] Romans 14:9

but he that believeth not is condemned already, because he hath not believed in the name of the only begotton Son of God."[a]

Notice the length of time from the slaying of the Passover lamb (Nisan 14) to the rescue from Egypt and the tyranny of Pharaoh (Nisan 17) and also to the next-day celebration of their completed redemption (Nisan 18).

Now, compare these events and their timing to the Crucifixion of Jesus. We see Jesus' death, His three days in the grave, followed by the joyous Easter celebration of His Resurrection.

Other Pictures

Just to make sure we understand the significance of Nisan 17, God gave even more prepictures of this vital day of rescue from death.

Scripture tells us that Noah's Ark, containing the only survivors of the universal judgment flood, touched solid ground on **Nisan 17.**[b]

Again in Esther we see the entire nation of Jews being snatched from certain annihilation on God's special day of **Nisan 17!**[c]

---

[a] John 3:17-18

[b] Genesis 8:4. Mankind followed God's original civil calendar at this time which made Nisan the seventh month.

[c] A careful reading of Esther 3-7 especially 3:7, 12, 4:16, 5:1, 14, 6:1, 14 and 7:1, 2, 10 show Nisan 17 as the day of national rescue.

REVIEW OF FEAST OF FIRSTFRUITS
(BIKKURIM)

As thanks for the first harvest in their Promised Land, the Jews offered a sheaf of grain to the Lord. This special day came every year on the Sunday that followed the Saturday after Passover.

The first person ever to rise from the dead, never to die again, is Jesus Christ. Joyful Christians celebrate this harvest of Resurrection every year on Easter Sunday. The Bible actually calls Jesus "the Firstfruits from the dead."

CHAPTER 6
FEAST OF WEEKS (Feast #4)

SPRING			
NISAN 14	NISAN 15	SUN. AFTER SABBATH	50 DAYS LATER
Preparation for Passover	Unleavened Dinner	Firstfruits, Resurrection	Weeks, Pentecost

Fifty days after Firstfruits, the Jews offered two loaves of bread, baked with leaven, as a second offering to the Lord: "*Ye shall count unto you from the morrow after the sabbath from the day that ye brought the sheaf of the wave offerings [Feast of Firstfruits]: seven sabbaths shall be complete: Even unto the morrow after the seventh sabbath shall ye number fifty days...Ye shall bring out of your habitation two waveloaves...of fine flour...baked with leaven*" (*Leviticus 23:15-17*). This comprised a second harvest festival, but notice the use of leaven this time.

This information becomes particularly exciting to Christians when we recognize that the fifty-day celebration of the Feast of Weeks was known in the days of the New Testament as **Pentecost**. This name, Pentecost (which Christians revere because it was the day the Holy Spirit descended on believers), is derived from the Greek for **fiftieth**. Imagine, just as the Jews were offering the two loaves of bread to the Lord, God sent His Holy Spirit to live inside of His believers!

As Christians, the significance of this feast is best savored by reading John 14:25, 26 and Acts 2:1-47. In these verses Jesus promised that when He went back to heaven, He would send the Holy Spirit to all believers to empower and to guide them. The day of Pentecost is considered the birth of the New Testament Church.[a] Jesus said, *"But ye shall receive power, after that the Holy Ghost is come upon you: and ye shall be witnesses unto me both in Jerusalem, and in Judea, and in Samaria, and unto the uttermost part of the earth."*[b]

For the first time, both Jews and Gentiles would carry the gospel message from God. Later God mentions these two groups, but says He is God of both of them.[c]

What a thrill to fathom the deep symbolism of the Feast of Weeks. The two loaves offered to the Lord represent the birth of the New Testament Church comprised of both Jews and Gentiles.[d]

This prophetic meaning is taught by Victor Buksbazen in *The Feasts of Israel* who adds, "The three thousand Jewish believers were the spiritual firstfruits of the church of Christ. Thus the Old Testament symbol, the two wave-loaves, became a glorious reality in the New—**a church composed of Jewish and Gentile believers,** purchased by the blood of the Lamb."[50]

---

[a] The "Church" means "the called out ones."

[b] Acts 1:8

[c] Romans 3:29

[d] The command for two loaves to represent the Church rather than a single loaf strengthens the promises of God to the nation of Israel. Although the Church is Jew and Gentile combined into a single group, God still remembers His chosen people. Romans, chapter 11 teaches that Israel is the olive tree and the Gentiles are grafted-in branches. One day this special time of the Church on earth will be over and the spotlight of God will once again be shining upon the olive tree (Jewish nation).

Could God's inclusion of leaven in this bread be representative of seeing this new group as including some error?

The bread of the Passover contained no leaven because it is a picture of perfect Jesus whose body was broken for us.[a] The leavened bread, however, may picture the Church which is not without error, even though we are forgiven. Note, *"Who shall change our vile bodies?"*[b] as well as Paul's accurate description of our remaining weakness to sin, *"For the good that I would I do not; but the evil which I would not that I do. Now if I do that I would not, it is no more I that do it, but sin that dwelleth in me."*[c] Scofield's notes state, "Leaven is present, because there is evil in the church."[d51]

Once again, a beautiful prophetic picture of God unfurls:

• The Feast of Weeks and the day of Pentecost occur fifty days after Firstfruits.

• The two loaves combined into one offering reminds us of Jews and Gentiles both being included in the New Testament Church.

• The leaven in the loaves reminds us that the members of the Church are not without sin.

---

[a] I Corinthians 11:24

[b] Philippians 3;20, 21

[c] Romans 7:19, 20

[d] Matthew 13:13; Acts 5:1,10; 15:1

An Interesting Probability

To Jewish writers, the giving of the Law on Mount Sinai is known as "the espousal of Israel to God."[a]

Note the scriptural tie-in of the wilderness journey to espousal. *"Go and cry in the ears of Jerusalem, saying Thus saith the Lord; I remember thee, the kindness of thy youth, the love of thine espousals, when thou wentest after me in the wilderness, in a land that was not sown. Israel was holiness unto the Lord, and the firstfruits of his increase."*[b]

According to Jewish historians, "A new theme was added to the festival of Shavuot after the destruction of the Temple in A.D. 70."[52]   The rabbis began to teach that Moses received the Law on Mount Sinai exactly fifty days after the Jews crossed the Red Sea, following their exit from Egypt.

Actually, the exact time of the giving of the Law, to the day, is hard to prove conclusively from the Bible. However, Scripture does give us excellent indications of the time gap between the Exodus and the giving of the Law.

As previously shown, the Jews killed the Passover lamb on Nisan 14, left Egypt on Nisan 15, passed through the Red Sea on Nisan 17, and celebrated their redemption on the Nisan 18. We can count from the day the Jews celebrated their new life of freedom until the day indicated

---

[a] Jewish belief is that, "God as the bride's father gives as dowry the 613 commandments, the Bible, Talmud and other sacred writings. Moses presents as dowry to his son — the people of Israel — the prayer shawl and phylacteries, the Sabbath and festivals. The contracts are witnessed by God and his servant Moses" (Najara Israel in *The Shavuot Anthology* by Philip Goodman).

[b] Jeremiah 2:2, 3

in the Bible that they reached the area of Mount Sinai to calculate the days that had transpired.

Scripture states, "*In the third month, when the children of Israel were gone forth out of the land of Egypt, the same day they came into the wilderness of Sinai.*"[a] In the Hebrew text the word translated "same" gives the indication that it was the third day as well as the third month. The number of days from the first month[b] (Nisan 18—their rescue from bondage in Egypt) to the third day of the third month (their arrival in the wilderness of Sinai) would be forty-six days.

The Lord then told Moses to prepare for the third day on which God himself will come down in the sight of the people on Mount Sinai. Moses went up the mountain and received laws for the Jews to live by as well as a verbal list of the Ten Commandments.

This sequence of events reasonably places the giving of the Law to the children of Israel on the fiftieth day after their rescue from Egypt. (The Feast of Weeks—also known as Shavuot or Pentecost—is celebrated, as mentioned, on the fiftieth day after Firstfruits.)

Interestingly, extra-biblical sources (besides rabbis) such as Falashas[c] and the book of Jubilees[d] also state that the Law was given on Shavuot (Feast of Weeks).[53]

Although it's hard to know conclusively from the Scriptures listed in this study that the Law was given on Mount Sinai on the fifty-day Feast of Weeks, the parallel

---

[a] Exodus 19:1

[b] Exodus 12:1

[c] Jews of Ethiopia.

[d] Second century B.C.

meanings of the events are amazing! An in-depth comparison of these two occurrences is done by Danny Litvin in *Pentecost Is Jewish.*[54]

By comparing Exodus 19:16-19 to Acts 2:2-15, Litvin points out the similarities between the giving of the Law and Pentecost. "The parallels are many: the time of day, the type of sound that was heard, the reaction of the people, the fire representing God, and the location—the central point for the Jewish people."

He goes on to show that the purposes of both the Law and the Holy Spirit were the same. They both give direction to mankind as to how to live life in the way God requires, convict mankind of sin and guilt, keep the believers separated from the world, mark those who belong to God, and point to God the Father.[55]

Because of the intricate skill God uses in weaving messages into the fabric of His word, this premise is probably true.

However, the wondrous truth we do know is that **the Jewish Feast of Weeks is Pentecost, the birth of the Church!**

REVIEW OF FEAST OF WEEKS (SHAVUOT)

Seven weeks and one day (fifty days) after the harvest celebration of Firstfruits, the Jews celebrated the Feast of Weeks. Part of this feast involved offering the Lord two loaves of bread, baked with leaven. This commemorated a second harvest and again the Jews thanked God for His provisions.

Forty days after Jesus Christ's Resurrection, He ascended into Heaven. Ten days after this ascension, just as the Jews were celebrating Pentecost (Feast of Weeks), God fulfilled a promise made by Jesus. On this very day the new believers gathered in Jerusalem and received the indwelling of the promised Holy Spirit.

This extraordinary event marks the birth of the Church. God tells us that the Church is made up of both Jews and Gentiles. Although Jesus can be represented by unleavened bread, mankind cannot. The two loaves with leaven represent Jews and Gentiles alongside each other as a worship offering to the Lord.

✡ ✡ ✡ ✡ ✡ ✡

SECTION III
FEAST DAYS YET UNFULFILLED

Interestingly, the four preceding Jewish spring feasts prepicture events connected with the first coming of Jesus.

After the fourth feast, which is a harvest festival, a notable time gap of nearly four months elapses before the remaining three feasts transpire in the autumn. The first of these fall celebrations is yet another harvest festival.

God describes these two harvest times as the "former" and the "latter" rain. How significant that God also uses these two times of rain to depict the first and second coming of Jesus![56]

Jesus makes reference to this gap between harvests after His encounter with the Samaritan woman. In speaking to His disciples concerning the importance of going to everyone with the gospel he warns, *"Say not ye, There are yet four months, and then cometh harvest? Behold, I say unto you, lift up your eyes, and look on the fields; for they are white already to harvest."*[a]

Was Jesus using this four month gap as a picture of the believer's responsibility during the Church age (the time

---

[a] John 4:35

between His first and second coming) to "*Go ye therefore, and teach all nations*" as recorded in Matthew 28:19?

Could this gap also be the two days[a] mentioned in Hosea after which God will revive the nation of Israel? Hosea describes God punishing the Jews for a time which lasts until "*they acknowledge their offence, and seek my face.*"[b] Are we to look for two twenty-four hour days to fulfill this prophecy of judgment or possibly two thousand years? Since the use of a number (two) shows us that a specific period of time is given, and since historically the Jews did not return to the Lord in two twenty-four hour days, perhaps the length of time intended in Hosea is two thousand years (garnered from the Scripture "*a thousand years as one day*").[c]

The Church Age is but a "parenthesis" in the total time period God has prescribed for the Jews. The beginning of this parenthesis, which initiated the Church Age, also denoted the suspension of the Jewish Era. Scripture reveals that this beginning parenthesis occurred on the Jewish Feast of Pentecost (Weeks).

The Rapture will complete the Church Age, marking the end of the parenthesis and the resumption of the Jewish Era. The end of the parenthesis recommences Jewish time so most reasonably it would also occur on a Jewish feast day. Since upon this resumption of Jewish time the Church Age would simultaneously be completed,

---

[a] The Hebrew word for day, "yowm," has a variety of definitions. It not only can be referring to a twenty-four hour day, it can also denote part of a day, an age, a required season, or many other meanings. As with many other Hebrew words, the context determines its exact meaning.

[b] Hosea 5:15-6:2

[c] Psalm 90:4; II Peter 3:8

wouldn't this completion (Rapture) of necessity occur on a Jewish feast day?

The remaining three feasts fall in the month of Tishri. To the Jews the fifth feast, Rosh HaShanah, is the day of judgment; the sixth feast, Yom Kippur, is the day of atonement; and the seventh, Succoth, is the season of rejoicing. These three feasts have yet to see their New Testament fulfillment.

God was exact to the day in timing the events that the first four feasts represented:

- Passover depicted Christ's Crucifixion.

- Unleavened Bread pictured the purging of sin.

- Firstfruits foretold Jesus' Resurrection. *Ascencion to the Father*

- Weeks illustrated the birth of the Church.

Could we then expect the last three feasts not only to be pictures of coming events, but also to <u>occur on the same day of the year</u> as their ancient counterparts? Do these three last feasts represent the time Jesus calls His bride,[a] returns to the earth a second time, and sets up His earthly kingdom?

✡ ✡ ✡ ✡ ✡ ✡

---

[a] Some expositors feel that no event relating to the Church can be found in the Old Testament because the Church is "a mystery yet unrevealed." *See* chapter on "Hidden Information" for further discussion of the Church in the feasts.

CHAPTER 7
FEAST OF THE TRUMPETS (Feast #5)

SPRING				FALL
NISAN 14	NISAN 15	SUN. AFTER SABBATH	50 DAYS LATER	TISHRI 1
Preparation for Passover	Unleavened Dinner	Firstfruits, Resurrection	Weeks, Pentecost	Trumpets, Rapture

Today, this feast is called Rosh HaShanah by the Jews. It occurs almost four months after the Feast of Weeks, falling in September or October. God instructed them to celebrate a sabbath by a blowing of trumpets.

Leviticus 23:24 says *"In the Seventh month, in the first day of the month shall ye have a sabbath, a memorial of blowing of trumpets, an holy convocation."* Although no more details are given in the Bible as to how to execute this blowing, it's fascinating to study the way the Jews traditionally observe this day.

According to the Talmud (Jewish comments on the legal sections of the Torah), the Jews attached an additional day of observance to this feast. This apparently occurred around 500 B.C., about one thousand years after the guidelines in Leviticus were given.[57] Historically, this change came about because of the Rabbis' desire to make sure all the people realized the new moon had been spied so that Rosh HaShanah could be declared. Since this feast inaugurated the new year, they felt the necessity of a two- day celebration. Authentication of each month's beginning was determined by reports of witnesses who testified to seeing the new moon. In order to avoid the error of celebrating the feast one day early or of missing by one day, thus causing the whole year's calendar to be askew, they added an extra day. This decision also resulted from an expressed concern that Jews living in outlying districts might not hear the proclamation in time to celebrate.[58]

They began the celebration of this feast during the previous month by blowing a ram's horn trumpet for twenty-nine days. On the last day of the month the blowing stopped. Then on the first day of Tishri (Rosh HaShanah), one more blowing of the trumpet occurred. This blowing consisted of three distinct series (of thirty blasts each) which then concluded with a blowing of ten blasts. At the end of all these blowings, there was one last, long sounding of the trumpet. It was called "Teki'ah Gedolah" which means, "The Great Blowing."[59]

Trumpet blowing is mentioned more than fifty times in the Old Testament. Although this sound was used to lead the people and to precede announcements, "gathering the people" describes the main use of the shofar,[a] or trumpet blast.[b]

Although each of the seven months, Nisan through Tishri, was introduced on its first day by the blowing of a trumpet, this fifth feast became known as the "Day of Blowing" or "Yom Teruah" by the Jews. Selection of this

---

[a] Usually made from a ram's horn. Other trumpets were crafted from silver.

[b] Exodus 19:13-19; Joshua 6:1-16

name came from Numbers 29:1 which refers to this feast day as "a day of blowing the trumpets." Since Tishri, the month of this Feast, had become the first month on the Jewish civil calendar, the Jews later began to call this feast day "Rosh HaShanah" which means "the beginning of the year."

Amazing Information

An amazing fact emerges in the writings of Jewish theologians concerning Rosh HaShanah. They inform us that the shofar's message "was interpreted also as a symbol of the **last trump** and as the rallying call of Israel in its eternal battle for the Kingdom of God."[60] Interestingly this is not literally the last trumpet to be blown in the festivals of the Jews. There are more blowings yet to come, including a particularly important one on Yom Kippur.

This amazing symbolic reference to the "last trump" contains profound implications for the Christian student of prophecy! After we finish unfolding the Jewish view of this feast day, we will compare this special name for Rosh HaShanah to the New Testament Scriptures.

Several possible reasons arise as to why this festival day became known by the people as the "last trump" day. First of all this festival day which featured one hundred blasts of the trumpet[61] was the last festival month on the calendar given to the Jews in Leviticus.[62] Secondly, this day closed with a single long blast of the shofar that became louder and louder until it ended.[63] This long blast reminded the Jews of the sustained trumpet blast that increased in loudness when the Lord came down to Mount Sinai to speak to Moses.[a]

One teacher of Jewish information gives an excellent presentation on this aspect of Rosh HaShanah. He explains that the "last trump" idiom for this feast comes from the Jewish connection of the ram's horn (shofar) with the ram that replaced Isaac as a sacrifice.[b64] He explains that the Jews believed that the ram caught in the thicket represented Messiah. They also teach that the left horn of this ram became the shofar blown on Mount Sinai at the giving of the Law. This blowing of the ram's horn became known as the "first trump."

Later in the festival of Rosh HaShanah, the Jews again make a connection with the ram substituted for Isaac. Regarding this association, Abraham Bloch, highly acclaimed Jewish author, records "The offspring of Isaac will someday transgress my will, and I will judge them on Rosh HaShanah. Should they appeal to my leniency, I will recall the binding of Isaac and let them blow then the horn of this ram [which was substituted for Isaac]." [65]

The shofar blown on Rosh HaShanah is considered to be the right horn of the ram in the binding of Isaac. Because of this connection with the remaining horn of the ram, this festival day acquired the additional name of, the "last trump" day.[66]

The Jewish belief about Rosh HaShanah is that it is:

1. A day of judgment, a call for repentance, and a time of regathering for the nation. Jewish writers tell us, "Isaiah explicitly associated the sound of the shofar with an

---

[a] Exodus 19:19

[b] Genesis 22:1-14

admonition against sin. *'Cry aloud, spare not, lift up your voice like a shofar, and declare unto my people their transgression, and to the house of Jacob their sin.'*(Isaiah 58:1) **The ingathering of the Jewish people and its ultimate return to God will be announced by a prolonged blast of the shofar.**[a] *'And it will come to pass in that day that a great shofar shall be blown, and they shall come that were lost in the land of Assyria, and they that were dispersed in the land of Egypt, and they shall worship the Lord in the holy mountain in Jerusalem'*(Isaiah 27:13)."[67]

2. A day of judgment for **all people.**[b] "Man is judged on Rosh HaShanah, and the verdict is sealed on Yom Kippur."[68] The Talmud states, "At the new year all creatures pass before him like sheep, as it is stated: He that fashions the heart of them all, that considers all their doings."[69]

3. A day "to confound and to confuse Satan, who the rabbis thought had a special predilection of accusing Israel on New Year's day, bringing up before the Lord all their shortcomings and sins."[70]

An Exciting Picture

When one looks at the verses that describe the Rapture, there is a fascinating similarity to the Feast of the Trumpets. In I Thessalonians 4:16-18, we are taught that Jesus will come for the believers *"with the trump of God."* More specifically, Paul wrote concerning the Rapture in I

---

[a] Emphasis mine.

[b] Emphasis mine.

Corinthians 15:51, 52, *"Behold, I show you a mystery; We shall not all sleep, but we shall all be changed, In a moment in the twinkling of an eye, <u>at the last trump:</u> for the trumpet shall sound, and the dead in Christ shall be raised incorruptible, and we shall be changed."*   (the 100th?

For nearly two thousand years the believers in Christ have quoted these words of promise with excitement. ?. How strange that we could so lovingly cherish each word of this special promise yet never once ask ourselves why Paul referred to the trumpet blast as "the last trump." We know that literally this is not the last trumpet to blow in the revealed plan of God.[a] In fact there are many more trumpet sounds yet to follow as recorded for us in the book of Revelation.

Could it be that the Hebrew believers of the first-century quite easily understood this "last trump" reference to be Rosh HaShanah because they understood the Jewish festivals and the different names by which they were known? This may be an example of how the lack of in-depth study of the Jewish holy days has caused many Christians throughout the centuries to miss important prophetic information in the Bible.

Since the Rapture is a gathering of believers and since the trumpet in the Old Testament was used primarily for gathering the people, let's consider the possibility that Rosh HaShanah may actually be the **day of the year** that the Rapture occurs.

---

[a] Some have taken this "last trump" blowing to be the last of the seven trumpet blasts in Revelation, chapter 11. However, since the use of trumpet blasts is essentially Jewish, it is necessary to interpret their meaning in light of Jewish understanding.

According to all Jewish theology the "Last Trumpet" blast during Rosh HaShanah is by no means the last use of trumpets during the seven festivals. The holy day of Yom Kippur ends with a blowing called the "Great Trumpet blast" (as outlined in the chapter on Yom Kippur).

The Great Gathering

Following the escape from Egypt and the return to the Promised Land, Jews have looked back to their rescue in celebration and praise. But God prophesies a rescue coming yet in the future that will completely overshadow this remembrance: *"Therefore, behold, the days come, saith the LORD, that it shall no more be said, The LORD liveth, that brought up the children of Israel out of the land of Egypt; But, The LORD liveth, that brought up the children of Israel from the land of the north, and from all the lands whither he had driven them: and I will bring them again into their land that I gave unto their fathers."*[a]

In the early 1900's, a number of Christian scholars suggested that the Trumpet Feast was the call for Israel to regather.[71] However, today most scholars agree that although it is obvious that God assisted the Jews in regaining ownership of Israel, we have not yet seen the true "regathering." To understand their reasoning one only needs to observe that even though the Jews once again possess their homeland, only four and one half million of the world's (perhaps) seventeen million Jews live in Israel.

Devotees of Bible prophecy were correct to thrill in 1948 when the land of Israel gained international recognition as the homeland of the Jews. However, this return was more of a restoration of the land than a fulfillment of the prophesied "regathering."[b] This restoration needed to transpire in order to 1) prepare the land to be occupied by a huge nation of people by the end

---

[a]   Jeremiah 16:14, 15

[b]   *See* Isaiah 18:3, 27:13, 58:1-14, and the book of Joel.

of the seven-year Tribulation and 2) set in power a Jewish state with whom the Antichrist could make a peace pact.

The Bible indicates this Antichrist's powerful take-over transpires after the Rapture.[a] The world acceptance of his control comes because of his promises of universal peace.[b] According to prophecy he actually stands behind a covenant guaranteeing peace to Israel.[c] Unfortunately, this long-awaited hope of peace is soon shattered as this evil, satanically-led dictator breaks the treaty after three and one-half years and attempts to annihilate the unsuspecting Jews.[d]

Preparation for Treaty

One needs only to read any issue of the *Jerusalem Post* to recognize the growing fear among European Jews as to their safety. The warnings of seasoned sufferers of prejudice caution that the growing undercurrent of anti-Semitism both in Europe and elsewhere is leading to another "holocaust."

As Israeli leaders struggle with the problems of housing shortages, inflation, and jobless citizens, "Aliya"[e] continues. The frantic immigration in 1990 alone moved 200,000 Jews to this tiny country.

---

[a] II Thessalonians 2:3-9

[b] Revelation 6:1, 2 and all of chapter 13

[c] More details on Antichrist's treaty are given in chapter on Hanukkah.

[d] Daniel 9:27; Revelation 12:13-17

[e] Term for Jewish immigration to Israel.

In 1991, 145,000 new Jews arrived. Unbelievably, in only one 24-hour period, the Israeli government welcomed 14,400 new immigrants! This project, Operation Solomon, brought nearly every Jew in Ethiopia to Israel. In the years succeeding 1991, immigration has dropped to about half of the 1991 level. No one knows how many will come during the nineties. The movement depends on the political climate around the world which stirs Jewry's recognition and fear of the smoldering anti-Semitic danger.

The greatest influx of immigrants into Israel has been from the old Soviet Union. Soviet Jews came for religious reasons during the seventies. The eighties brought the "refusnicks" while the immigrants of the nineties come primarily for a better life. Most of these only know they are Jews because of the big "Y" standing for Yid on their identity card. This "Y" is reminiscent of the yellow star Jews had to wear in Nazi Germany. Even in Russia today the "Y" makes keeping a job or finding an apartment difficult. This influx has swollen the percentage of Russian Jews in Israel to 10 percent of the total population.

It's noteworthy to recognize that most Gentiles are not supportive of Israel nor (historically) have Jews been very welcome in Gentile nations. How interesting to note that the people who are the exceptions to the ongoing criticism and abuse of Jews are mostly pre-millennial, evangelical Christians.[a][72]

Most likely, when authentic Christians leave in the Rapture, **there will be no safe country, no safe place left for the Jews of the world, except Israel!** This heavenly withdrawal of a host of Jewish supporters will only

---

[a] This point is mentioned even by the Jews themselves in comments in the *Jerusalem Post*. They comment that those who take a literal interpretation of the Bible as opposed to an allegorical approach comprise the bulk of the Christian support for Jews.

compound the dangers of both worldwide anti-Semitism and the historic Arab-Israeli conflict. This unstable condition arising from multiple problems will pave the way for complete Jewish acceptance of a world peace treaty.

Interesting Jewish Insights Concerning Rosh HaShanah

Rabbis emphasize the joyous character of Rosh HaShanah as well as its solemnity.[73] Three stages of judgment are seen by Jewish scholars: "Three books are opened on Rosh HaShanah, one for the wicked, one for the righteous, and one for the in-between. The righteous are immediately inscribed in the book of life, the wicked in the book of death, and the verdict of the in-between is suspended until Yom Kippur."[74] The scriptural origin of this belief comes from God's statement, *"And I will cause you to pass under the rod, and I will bring you into the land of the covenant."*[a]

Could the righteous people they see be the believers, both Jewish and Gentile, who are taken up in the Rapture? Since Rosh HaShanah is a harvest festival, this day may well represent the harvest of souls taken up to heaven. Remember at Firstfruits four months earlier, one sheaf was waved but it is referred to both in Leviticus and I Corinthians in the **plural**. *"Christ the firstfruits; afterward they that are Christ's at His coming."*[b] Using the plural makes

---

[a]   Ezekiel 20:37. The reference to "passing under the rod" comes from the shepherd's practice of sorting the sheep that come into the fold at night as the sheep pass under the shepherd's rod.

[b]   I Corinthians 15:23

the picture complete. Firstfruits represented Jesus first,
then it represents all believers for whom He provides His
righteousness and salvation.

Perhaps the wicked who are inscribed in the book of
the dead are those referred to in the book of Revelation as
having taken the mark of the beast during Tribulation.
*"And all that dwell upon the earth shall worship him, whose
names are not written in the book of life of the Lamb slain from
the foundation of the world." "And the smoke of their torment
ascendeth up for ever and ever: and they have no rest day nor
night, who worship the beast and his image, and whosoever
receiveth the mark of his name." "And they that dwell on the
earth shall wonder, whose names were not written in the book of
life from the foundation of the world."*[a]

Maybe the last group referred to as the "in-betweens"
are those who do not take the mark of the beast, and will
(during or at the end of the seven years of Tribulation) at
last believe in Jesus Christ as Messiah![b]

REVIEW OF FEAST OF TRUMPETS
(ROSH HASHANAH)

The all-day blowing of trumpets ushered in this Jewish
feast day. This first day of the Jewish year is celebrated as
a solemn day of gathering, examination by God, and
confounding of Satan. The last trumpet blast of this Rosh
HaShanah gathering beautifully describes the focal point
of Christian hope, the Rapture!

---

[a] Revelation 13:8, 14:11, 17:8

[b] Zechariah 12:8:10; Revelation 7:3-8, 14:1-5

CHAPTER 8
DAY OF ATONEMENT (Feast #6)

SPRING				FALL	
NISAN 14	NISAN 15	SUN. AFTER SABBATH	50 DAYS LATER	TISHRI 1	TISHRI 10
Preparation for Passover	Unleavened Dinner	Firstfruits, Resurrection	Weeks, Pentecost	Trumpets, Rapture	Atonement, 2nd coming

The most solemn holy day of the Jews today is known as Yom Kippur. On this day, the ordinary transactions of life in Israel stop completely. The deserted streets and closed switchboards demonstrate that all the people have only one thought in mind, the celebration of Yom Kippur.

As originally given by God, the ritual could begin only after the high priest offered a bullock as a sin offering for himself and his family. God then instructed him to select two goats. By a drawing of lots, one was selected as a sacrifice offering for the sins of the nation of Israel. The high priest carried the blood of this goat into the Holy of Holies and sprinkled it on and in front of the Mercy Seat.

The nation waited in hushed anticipation as their high priest came out of the holy place and sprinkled the blood of the bullock and the goat upon the horns of the altar seven times. If the priest lived through the whole ritual, the nation knew God had forgiven them for one more year!

Next, the high priest called for the second goat, placed his hands on its head, and confessed over it the sins of the nation. A priest then led it out to the wilderness and let it go.[a] This scapegoat, called "Azazel" in Hebrew, figuratively bore the sins of the people.

The Jews traditionally ended this solemn celebration by a blowing of the shofar horn called "Shofar haGadol" or "The Great Trumpet." This blowing symbolized not only the end of the ceremony, but gaiety, since the national, yearly sacrifice had been accepted.[75]

Victor Buksbazen writes in *The Gospel in the Feasts of Israel* that the Jews believe, "On Yom Kippur God seals the books of accounting which have been opened on New Year's Day. Whereas before on New Year's Day, (Rosh HaShanah) Jews wish one another that their name be 'inscribed' into the book of life, in the days leading up to the Day of Atonement, when greeting one another or sending greetings in writing, the word is 'may you be sealed in the book of life.'"[76] Although the Day of Atonement is the tenth day of the seventh month, the preceding seven days have become connected to this feast. These seven days are called by the Jews, "The Days of Affliction" or "The Days of Awe."

On the first day of these seven (the third of Tishri), the Fast of Gedaliah is observed. The next observance during these seven days is called "Shabbat Shuvah," which is held on the Sabbath (Saturday) of this week. The last special day of these seven Days of Awe is called "Erev Yom

---

[a] Leviticus 16:1-34

Kippur" or Yom Kippur Eve. Instructions for Yom Kippur command the Jews to "*afflict your souls by a statute forever.*"ᵃ

The Jews today still afflict themselves on Erev Yom Kippur. They confess their sins and recite, "For He is merciful and forgives iniquity." Only after this total week of soul-searching does the all-important Day of Atonement begin.

Handling the Loss of the Temple

The biblical guidelines for Yom Kippur were observed by the Jews as long as they had the Tabernacle or the Temple in which to properly offer the sacrifices. After the destruction of Herod's Temple in A.D. 70, the Jews faced the question of how to celebrate this religious service.

The rabbinic leadership experienced tremendous shock as a result of losing their Temple. The depth of their loss is reflected in their dismal words. "Now that we have no prophet or Kohen or sacrifice, who shall atone for us? The only thing left to us is prayer."[77]

They also say, "Prayer was a natural substitute for the sacrificial offerings...Subsequently, the rabbis added two more keys to salvation, **essential to winning God's mercies on Yom Kippur.**"ᵇ

"Said Rabbi Eliezerᶜ: 'Three elements avert a harsh decree, they are—prayer, charity, and penitence.'"[78]

ᵃ Leviticus 16:29-31 Jews believe this is God's appointed time to become introspective and search for any sins yet unconfessed. Some Jews even have interpreted this instruction to mean physical flagellation.

ᵇ Emphasis mine.

ᶜ Respected second century rabbi.

They base these three replacement choices on Hosea 12:2,3 and Nehemiah 8:9.

It's amazing to see the direction this theology has taken the Jewish beliefs which, as you will see, is far afield from the original design of Yom Kippur. **Confession of sin to God and a God-ordained substitutionary blood sacrifice has been replaced by a man-centered, good works system of appeasement toward God.**

This drastic shift is substantiated by a contemporary Jewish theologian who writes, "The rabbinic three keys to salvation emphasized the social aspects of Yom Kippur. Whereas the previous sacrificial motif of the fast was mainly God-directed, the rabbinic orientation gave concrete emphasis to the prophetic admonitions that man's protestations of piety are not acceptable to God if his sense of social justice is faulty. To obtain divine forgiveness, one must not only make peace with God, but also man. The attainment of peace, individual and communal, thus became a prime objective of Yom Kippur. It is in this spirit that Rabbi Eleazar[a] declared: 'Great peace, for **even if Israel is worshiping idols,**[b] if they keep the peace and are united, they will be spared the judgment of the Almighty'(Pesikta Rabbati)."[79]

This works-centered justification system is certainly in contradiction to the Jews' own commentary on the Bible, the Talmud. It states, "*There is no atonement except with blood.*"[80]

A detailed reading of the sacrificial rites was incorporated as part of the Yom Kippur liturgy. Still today, these three elements of prayer, charity, and penitence are

---

[a] A contemporary of Rabbi Eliezer.

[b] Emphasis mine.

the replacements for the once-a-year national blood sacrifice. Only the ritual of Kapparot retains any semblance to the original Yom Kippur sacrifices. Some Orthodox Jews select a chicken, preferably white, and recite, "A life for a life." After prayers and a laying of their right hand upon the head of the "kapparah," they swing this live chicken over their head and say, "This is my substitute, this is my exchange, this is my atonement. This fowl will go to death, and I shall enter upon a good and long life and peace." After three repetitions of this ceremony the chicken is slaughtered.[81]

The loss of the Temple and the opportunity to offer sacrifice to God brought the Jews to a fork in the road. They could take the path of redesigning their approach to God, or follow the other road by asking themselves the question, "If God has allowed the destruction of our only place of sacrifice, has He perhaps already provided the promised sacrifice of Isaiah 53?"

The Ultimate Prophecy

Hundreds of prophesies in the Tanakh[a] pointed to Jesus as the ultimate messianic sacrifice. Isaiah chapter 53 typifies this information. But even beyond the Old Testament prophesies and the flawless life of Jesus, God gave another messianic indicator. This phenomenon was directly related to the Temple worship and particularly to Yom Kippur.

Between the Holy Place and the Holy of Holies hung an elaborate curtain called "the veil." Its name in Hebrew means "to hide or cover." This blue, purple, and scarlet veil of fine-twined, byssus linen, glittered with the woven-

---

[a] All of the Old Testament.

gold figures of cherubim. The purpose of the veil was twofold. Besides shielding the Holy of Holies from all but the high priest, this veil covered the Ark whenever the Jews relocated[a] their portable Temple[b].

J. Vernon McGee comments on the veil in *The Tabernacle: God's Portrait of Christ*: "It protected the holiness of God, whether on the wilderness march or when it was in its place in the Tabernacle. It protected the holiness of God from the profanity of man. It protected both God and man.

"When the Temple of Solomon was erected, the veil was perpetuated in the Temple, only it was larger and more elaborate. It was a beautiful work of art, gorgeous in design, artistic in color, superb in the minutest detail, and rich in adornment... Josephus tells us that it was **four inches thick** in his day and renewed each year. **Wild horses tied to each end of the veil, after it had been taken down, were not able to rend it asunder.**"[c] [82]

A cascade of astonishing phenomena struck Jerusalem at the exact moment of Jesus' death. An earthquake shook the city. Rocks split apart. Inside the Temple, though, an even more awesome event, heavy with significance, touched the veil. This curtain, four inches thick, was **ripped from top to bottom** by an unseen hand.

Matthew solemnly describes this awesome event. *"Jesus, when he had cried again with a loud voice, yielded up the ghost. And, behold the veil of the temple was rent in twain from*

---

[a] Numbers 4:5

[b] Known as the Tabernacle and used from Moses until Solomon.

[c] This actually took place in A.D. 70. The Roman army destroyed everything in the Temple and leveled the building leaving not even a brick standing.

the top to the bottom; and the earth did quake, and the rocks rent."[a]

The veil no longer separated the people from the Holy of Holies. What did this mean? What about Yom Kippur? God answers these questions by explaining that Jesus became the "*once for all*" Yom Kippur sacrifice. God promises, "*By one offering he hath perfected for ever them that are sanctified...And their sins and iniquities will I remember no more...Now where remission of these is, there is no more offering for sin...Having therefore, brethren, boldness to enter into the holiest by the blood of Jesus...By a new and living way, which he hath consecrated for us, through the veil, that is to say, his flesh.*"[b]

This veil had been a forerunner, an Old Testament picture of Jesus Christ. For fifteen hundred years, access to the glory and forgiveness of God had been provided only one way, via a priest, through the veil. God ripped the veil in half at the moment of Jesus' death. As on previous Yom Kippurs, God accepted the sacrifice, but this time it was forever. It never needed to be repeated again. Jesus became the access to God, so the separating curtain was replaced by the Holy Person of the Godhead whom it represented.

Some Jews and some Gentiles recognized the fulfillment of Old Testament prophecy in the person of Jesus Christ. Most did not. History and the rabbinical teachings demonstrate a choice to refuse God's plan which offered Jesus as fulfilling the need for the shedding of innocent blood. Instead they invented a works system of approach to God.

---

[a] Matthew 27:50, 51

[b] Hebrews 10:10, 14, 17-22

Certainly the Jews are not alone in the attempt to approach God on the basis of their deeds instead of on the basis of the substitutionary sacrifice of Jesus. Mankind at large makes the same exchange by the religions which they design. Sadly a works system is even taught by many who claim the name of "Christian."

God reaffirmed the Old Testament teaching concerning the absolute necessity of a blood sacrifice. He stated in the New Testament, *"Without the shedding of blood there is no remission of sins."* How sad that today numbers of so-called Christians as well as many Jews find the references to blood sacrifice "barbaric."

Solemn words from God warn us about this independent attitude. *"There is a way that seemeth right unto man, but the end thereof are the ways of death."*[a] Oh how much need there is for each one of us to say the words of Acts 5:29, *"We ought to obey God rather than man."*

Yom Kippur's Picture

God commanded concerning Yom Kippur, *"And this shall be an everlasting statute unto you, to make an atonement for the children of Israel for all their sin once a year."*[b]

Just before the prophetic picture (Isaiah 53) of the Messiah who would die for the sins of the nation, another picture of Yom Kippur occurs. Isaiah prophesies, *"As many were astonished at thee; his visage was so marred more than any man, and his form more than the sons of men; so shall he sprinkle*

---

[a] Proverbs 16:25

[b] Leviticus 7:25

many nations."[a] This mention of "sprinkling" is a direct reference to the sprinkling on the altar done by the high priest on Yom Kippur.

Believers in Jesus Christ, who have studied the New Testament, understand that the high priest's job of representing the nation was an early picture of the Great High Priest, Jesus Christ. The book of Hebrews in a reference to Jesus promises, *"Wherefore he is able to save them to the uttermost that come unto God by him, seeing he ever liveth to make intercession for them.*

For such an high priest became us, who is holy, harmless, undefiled, separate from sinners, and made higher than the heavens;

Who needeth not daily, as those high priests, to offer up sacrifices, first for his own sins, and then for the people's: for this he did once, when he offered up himself."[b]

The typology or picture concerning the Day of Atonement is further explained in Hebrews chapter 9.

The two goats used on Yom Kippur present a beautiful picture of Jesus. One goat had to die (as Jesus had to die) while the other goat lived and carried the sins of the people into the wilderness and disappeared. Jesus, as our living Savior, carries our sins, and God removes them from us, *"As far as the east is from the west."[c]*

It grieves us to discover that the observance of this feast was changed by the Jews sometime after the specifics had been given to them by God. By the second Temple

---

[a] Isaiah 52:14, 15

[b] Hebrews 7:25-27

[c] Psalm 103:12

period,ᵃ they were pulling hair out of the scapegoat and shouting angrily as it was led past them on the way to the desert. How amazing that this anger toward the goat, that was bearing their sins, so reflects the behavior of many Jews as Jesus was arrested, tried, and crucified for the sins of the world.

Strangely, someone designed a new ending to the ceremony of Yom Kippur. Jewish historian Theodor Gaster tells us the scapegoat, marked by a crimson thread, walked alongside a chosen priest to a ravine located twelve miles outside Jerusalem. Standing at the edge of the precipice, the priest divided the red thread, tying one part to a rock and the other between the horns of the goat. "Then he pushed the animal from behind till it went rolling down, 'and' says the Mishna, 'ere it reached half-way, it was broken to pieces.'"[83]

As we know, today the Jews do not have a living Savior. The prophetic importance in Yom Kippur is seen in both the original guidelines as given by God and in the changes the Jews instituted.

Another Tragic Change

God gave exact guidelines to Moses describing the dimensions for the Tabernacle as well as the objects to place inside. According to God's guidelines, the inner court, as well as the Holy of Holies, had no windows.[84] Priests could see to officiate within the inner court from the light provided by a golden lampstand. This light was to be kept burning continually.

The Holy of Holies, however, not only had no source of outside light, it also had no physical provision of light

---

ᵃ 515 B.C.

inside. The only object of furniture it contained was the Ark of the Covenant. This wooden box, covered inside and out with gold, contained a pot of manna,[a] Aaron's rod that budded, and the stone tablets of law.[b] The Mercy Seat of pure gold rested on the top, over which two golden cherubims hovered with wings outstretched.

(The significance of these objects as prepictures of Jesus Christ being the access to God is beautifully portrayed in J. Vernon McGee's book, *The Tabernacle: God's Portrait of Christ*.)

The Bible explains that after the craftsmen under Moses finished the tabernacle, "*The glory of the Lord filled the tabernacle.*"[c] Because of God's light, the high priest could see to carry out the yearly ritual of Yom Kippur.

This light of God is intricately involved with the Ark itself as demonstrated when the Ark was stolen by the Philistines. "*The glory is departed from Israel: because the ark of God was taken.*"[d] Not too surprisingly, after the Philistines were devastated by disease because they possessed the ark, and the Bethshemites lost 50,070 men for looking inside, the Ark was gladly returned. The Ark eventually rested in the permanent version of the Tabernacle, known as Solomon's Temple. Once again, God provided His light in the Holy of Holies.[e]

---

[a] Food that God provided the Jews during the forty year wandering in the desert.

[b] Hebrews 9:4, 5

[c] Exodus 40:34, 35

[d] I Samuel 4:21

[e] I Kings 8:11

Unfortunately, the Jews slowly ceased to worship and obey God which brought about the withdrawal of God's glory from the Temple and their eventual expulsion from the Promised Land.[a]

Babylonians destroyed Solomon's Temple in 587 B.C.[b] A second Temple built by Jews in 515 B.C., was refurbished and greatly enlarged, by Herod the Great in 19 B.C. This elaborate and enormous structure covered forty acres and took decades to complete. Jewish sources say the Holy of Holies in this Temple remained empty, apparently never possessing the ark.[85] Consequently, the glory of God never resided in this Temple!

The Tragic Change Occurs

Now let's look at the aforementioned tragic change in Yom Kippur. The *Encyclopedia Judaica* records a short statement containing profound implications. It states that on the three pilgrim festivals (which would include Yom Kippur) "the curtain which normally hung at the entrance to the sanctuary was rolled up to enable the people to view the Holy of Holies."[86]

The tragedy of this revelation is that not only did the Jews commit a sacrilege by looking inside the sanctuary, they state the reason they lifted the curtain was so the people outside could see in. Could it be that the lone

---

[a] Ezekiel 10:18-19

[b] J. Vernon McGee mentions the "ensign" that will come from Ethiopia (referred to in Isaiah 18:3) is a possible reference to the Ark of the Covenant *Isaiah vol. I* p.141.

Grant Jeffrey discusses in chapter VIII of his book, *Heaven: The Last Frontier,* the possibility that the Ark in Solomon's Temple was only a replica. He suggests that a secret exchange took place and that the original Ark was known to be absent from the second Temple. He also presents a fascinating scenario describing Ethiopia as the present location of the authentic Ark.

candelabra no longer gave sufficient light for the priests to officiate? What a tragedy! Even though the glory of God had long since departed, neither the people nor the priests noticed that God was no longer a part of this ceremony. On Yom Kippur, what mercy could the high priest hope to find for his nation in the dark and empty Holy of Holies?

This picture of turning from God, and not recognizing that His power had departed, is reminiscent of Samson's experience. After Samson turned his back on God and gave in to Delilah's pleadings to tell her the secret of his strength, the Bible says, "*He wist not that the Lord was departed from him.*"[a]

It's no wonder that the Pharisees who possessed this same spiritual blindness were referred to by Jesus as "*blind guides*" and "*whited sepulchres...full of dead men's bones.*"[b]

More Meaning

The Jewish custom of ten days of "Teshuvah"[c] begins on Rosh HaShanah and ends on Yom Kippur. Within this time their seven Days of Affliction present us with even more prophetic significance. Remember, beginning on the third of Tishri, the Fast of Gedaliah transpires. Nobel prize winner S.Y. Agnon tells us in *Days of Awe*, "Conscientious readers go into seclusion for seven days beginning with the Fast of Gedaliah until Yom Kippur, and study the order of service and mend their deeds and

---

[a] Judges 16:20

[b] Matthew 23:24, 27

[c] This Jewish belief defines a time of intense introspection when the sinner tries to recall all his sin, forsake it, and remove it from his thoughts concluding never to do it again. If he is faithful in his repentance, he will be forgiven on Yom Kippur.

seclude themselves to be alone with their Maker night and day in solitude and piety, as the high priest used to do."[87]

Note another aspect of Jewish teaching concerning the Days of Awe. "The Sabbath between Rosh HaShanah and Yom Kippur is called the 'Sabbath of Return,' because then the portion from the Prophets beginning 'Return O Israel, unto the Lord thy God' (Hosea 14:2) is read."[88]

It is very possible that the seven days during which the Jews prepare themselves spiritually for the Great Day of Atonement is God's picture of the seven-year great Tribulation.

Another correlation of Yom Kippur and the day of recognition of Jesus as Messiah is seen in the writing of a Jewish rabbi. Philip Goodman records an amazing act which ends this seven-day observance. On this last day (which is the Day of Atonement) the participants pronounce the "ineffable[a] name of God" and bow the knee at the feeling of God's nearness. "**Here and only here does the Jew kneel...The congregation prostrates itself before the King of Kings.**"[b][89]

We know God promises in the Old and New Testaments that on some future day every knee will bow before Him,[c] but how meaningful this observance becomes when the light of Philippians 2:10 shines upon it: "*That at the name of Jesus every knee shall bow.*" Yes, even the current observances of Jews reveal that much is already in place for national recognition of their Messiah, Jesus, on **some** Yom Kippur.

---

[a] Unutterable, never to be spoken except at this time.

[b] Emphasis mine.

[c] Isaiah 45:22-25; Romans 14:11

It is actually taught by the Jews that because of this face-to-face confrontation with God, the Jewish idiom for Yom Kippur became **"face to face"**![90] Do not those words simply leap out at us? In the light of a Jewish perspective of Yom Kippur we can savor the words, *"For now we see through a glass darkly; but then face to face."*[a]

The Great Trumpet Blast

The ceremonies of Yom Kippur close with the trumpet blast called Shofar haGadol. This great blast sounds upon the "closing of the gate" ceremony which formally ends Yom Kippur. How like God's words, *"And it shall come to pass in that day, that the great trumpet shall be blown, and they shall come which were ready to perish in the land of Assyria, and the outcasts in the land of Egypt, and shall worship the Lord in the holy mount at Jerusalem."*[b] God's word reveals information that ties in a great trumpet blast with the total regathering of the Jews to Israel and the Second Coming of Jesus.[c]

During this present Church age, the Lord has been dealing directly with mankind as a whole, rather than through the Jewish nation. After the Rapture of the Church (comprised of believing Gentiles and Jews), God will once again turn His spotlight on the nation of the Jews. God plans, through these seven years, to bring the Jews to a spiritual condition in which they at last

---

[a] I Corinthians 13:12

[b] Isaiah 27:13. Although Jewish writers connect this verse to Rosh HaShanah, the correct application of this Scripture can only be made when Jesus is recognized as Messiah.

[c] See Isaiah 18:3, 58:1; Joel 2:1, 15; Matthew 24:31

recognize the true identity of Jesus. I believe Yom Kippur will be the exact time the now-believing nation of Jews will bow before Jesus as their Messiah. This future turning to God is described in chapters 12 and 14 of Zechariah. *"And I will pour out upon the house of David, and upon the inhabitants of Jerusalem, the spirit of grace and of supplication: and they shall look upon me whom they have pierced, and they shall mourn for him, as one mourneth for his only son, and shall be in bitterness for him as one that is in bitterness for his firstborn."*[a]

How fitting that Jewish custom teaches that this holy day is the time a person's name can be sealed in the book of life!

REVIEW OF THE DAY OF ATONEMENT (YOM KIPPUR)

The most solemn feast of the seven listed in Leviticus, is the Day of Atonement. On this day, known as Yom Kippur, hangs the fate of the whole nation of Israel. The high priest enters the Holy of Holies to offer a sacrifice for the sins of the nation. If the sacrifice is accepted by God, then the nation of Jews rejoices because they have been given another year to live.

Since the loss of the Temple in A.D. 70, it has been impossible to celebrate this feast according to God's original design.

One gazes in amazement at the awesome picture of redemption contained in Yom Kippur. Jesus Christ, as mankind's great High Priest, entered the Holy of Holies in heaven to present His sacrificial blood to God the Father.

---

[a] Zechariah 12:10

God's acceptance of this offering provided eternal salvation for all who trust in Christ's sacrifice.

CHAPTER 9
FEAST OF TABERNACLES
(Feast #7)

SPRING				FALL		
NISAN 14	NISAN 15	SUN. AFTER SABBATH	50 DAYS LATER	TISHRI 1	TISHRI 10	TISHRI 15
Preparation for Passover	Unleavened Dinner	Firstfruits, Resurrection	Weeks, Pentecost	Trumpets, Rapture	Atonement, 2nd coming	Tabernacles, Millennium

Succoth, or Festival of Tabernacles (Booths), is an eight day time of joyous commemoration. At this time the Jews remember and thank the Lord for the provisions He gave them after they were rescued from bondage in Egypt.

According to the instructions in Leviticus chapter 23, the Jews celebrated this feast by building booths of palm, willow, and other thick branches. For the first seven days, special offerings burned on the altar.[91] Later, they added the ceremonies of the pouring of water and the lighting of four huge elevated lamps in the Temple courtyard. These symbols reminded the Jews of God's provision of water in the wilderness and of His pillar of fire that guided them by night. Four huge oil-burning vats actually beamed shafts of light across the whole city of Jerusalem.

The water-pouring ceremony, repeated on each of the seven days, brought such great joy to the people that Succoth became known as "the season of our joy." The celebrants each brought an "etrog" or citron—the yellow, lemon sized, sweet and spicy citrus fruit. Besides bringing this fruit as suggested in Leviticus, the jubilant participants wove branches of palm, myrtle, and willow into a large fan called a "lulav."

Meanwhile the priests divided themselves into three large groups, each group heading in a different direction. One group set off to Bethlehem to purchase animals for the day's sacrifice. Another group traveled in procession from the Temple to a place below Jerusalem called Motza where they cut off willow branches. These priests returned in a long line, all waving these tall limbs back and forth. The third contingent of priests exited through the water gate taking with them a golden flagon. The high priest dipped out three measures of water from the pool of Siloam then returned leading his group of priests.

Back in Time

Calling this festival "season of our joy" can readily be understood when we take ourselves back in time for a moment to listen and observe this awesome spectacle...

Look at the long line of priests, hundreds of them, threading through the water gate and winding down to the pool of Siloam. More priests curl through the narrow streets on the way to Bethlehem to secure the special sacrifices. Gaze across the holy city and see hundreds of thousands of Jewish pilgrims lining the streets waving their lulavs. Not to be overlooked, watch the column of priests waving their huge willow branches as they return through the eastern gate to the Temple.

The sound, oh the glorious sound. Hear the heavenly sound of the flute. Listen to the Levites on the Temple steps. How many are there? They're playing flutes and lyres, cymbals and trumpets. Oh the joy! Listen to the people! Hear them singing the words of the psalms. *"Praise ye the Lord. Blessed is the man that feareth the Lord...This is the Lord's doing; it is marvelous in our eyes. This is the day which the Lord hath made; we will rejoice and be glad in it."*[a]

The climactic ending came each day when the three lines of priests converged at the altar. First they placed the sacrifices upon the altar. Next the willow-bearing priests placed their cut branches around the altar forming a circle that canopied the animals. Last the high priest, carrying the golden flagon of water, ascended the steps leading to the altar. Connected to the altar were two plaster, funnel-shaped bowls with tubes below that ran back into the altar. Each day's ceremony ended with the high priest pouring his measures of water into the bowl while his assistant poured measures of wine into the other bowl.[92]

Beginning one month before Rosh HaShanah (forty days before Yom Kippur), the worship and study of the Scriptures led up to these ceremonies. Every Scripture in these studies related to water and light, keeping the symbolism fresh in everyone's mind. They heard words such as, *"Behold God is my salvation; I will trust and not be afraid; for the Lord JEHOVAH is my strength and my song; he also is become my salvation. Therefore with joy shall ye draw water out of the wells of salvation."*[b]

---

[a] Psalms 112-118 were sung at Passover, Firstfruits, and Tabernacles.

[b] Isaiah 12:2, 3

Can't you feel the electricity and utter amazement of the thousands gathered in the Temple courtyard on the day that Jesus attended the Feast of Tabernacles? Imagine, He called out to the crowd, "*If any man thirst, let him come to Me, and drink. He that believeth on Me, as the scripture hath said, out of his belly shall flow rivers of living water.*"[a] He used this ceremony of the pouring of the water to offer His beloved people the salvation He had come to provide.

Doesn't the pouring out of the water and the wine remind us of the ultimate price of love Jesus paid for us on the cross? Remember one of the soldiers "*pierced his side, and forthwith came out blood and water.*"[b] He used this celebration which pictured Him so beautifully, not just in the water pouring but also in the branches,[c] then in the lambs, the rams, the bulls, and the goat, to reach out in love to His people.

At the end of this feast on its eighth day, Jesus again stunned the Pharisees when He used their ritual celebration of lights to teach that He was the Messiah. Standing in the very same courtyard that held the four great lights, he proclaimed, "*I am the light of the world: he that followeth me shall not walk in darkness, but shall have the light of life.*"[d]

---

[a] John 7:2, 10, 37-39

[b] John 19:34

[c] Isaiah 4:2; 11:1

[d] John 8:12

From the Past to the Future

In the Bible we discover that Solomon chose the Feast of Tabernacles to dedicate the first Temple.ᵃ This day of the year seems to be selected by God as His special time of consecration. The representation of Jesus in Feast of Tabernacles comes alive to us in a Jewish prayer repeated during the celebration. This petition added to the grace said after meals, asks, "May the All-merciful raise up for us the fallen Tabernacle (*succah*) of David."[93] A contemporary Jewish rabbi comments on this ancient prayer, "We ask for the restoration of the Davidic Kingdom, the Messianic Age."[94]

We see pictures of Jesus in this beautiful Jewish Succoth poem. It describes the remembrance of past provision in the wilderness as well as future hope of a Messianic Kingdom age.

> Thy cloud enfolded them, as if that they
> Were shelter'd in a booth; redeem'd and free,
> They saw Thy glory as a canopy
> Spread o'er them as they marched upon their way
>
> And when dryshod they through the sea had gone,
> They praised Thee and proclaimed Thy unity;
> And all the angels sang the antiphon,
> And lifted up their voices unto Thee.
> "Our Rock, our Savior He"—thus did they sing—
> "World without end, the Lord shall reign as King!"[95]

ᵃ I Kings 8:1-5; II Chronicles 7:8-10

Fulfillment of Tabernacles

Most Bible scholars are agreed on the future fulfillment of the Feast of Tabernacles. This is the Millennium![a] Jesus Christ will reign from Jerusalem. The whole world will look to the Jews for knowledge of the Lord.[b] Zechariah describes this exciting time for us. *"And it shall come to pass, that every one that is left of all the nations which came against Jerusalem shall even go up from year to year to worship the King, the Lord of hosts, and to keep the feast of Tabernacles."*[c]

From the sacred writings of the Jews we read these amazing words that describe the rehearsal for this coming era. "The people said to the nations of the earth: Because of us, the Holy One blessed be He, does all these [good] things for you, and yet you hate us...At the Festival of Tabernacles we offer up seventy bullocks [as an atonement] for the seventy nations, and we pray that rain will come down for them."[96]

How fascinating to note in a previously quoted passage of Hosea[d], that not only is a time of two thousand years of judgment indicated for the Jewish nation, but this passage also infers that afterwards, a one thousand year peaceful reign of Messiah will transpire for the Jews. The passage states, *"After two days will he revive us: in the third day he will raise us up, and we shall live in his sight."*

---

[a] Revelation 20:4-6

[b] Zechariah 8:23

[c] Zechariah 14:16, see also verses 4, 9

[d] Hosea 5:12-6:3

REVIEW OF FEAST OF TABERNACLES (SUCCOTH)

Celebrating Tabernacles in Israel produces jubilation throughout their land. Festivities surround this remembrance of God's provision during the wandering in the wilderness and the future hope of a messianic kingdom of peace. Each family enjoys the relaxation in the booths of branches built on their rooftops[a] and balconies or in their yards.

The prophetic masterpiece, painted by God in the Feast of Tabernacles, is none other than the peaceful, future one thousand year reign of Jesus Christ.

After observing the prophetic meaning of all seven Jewish feasts, the Hebrew definition of "feasts" becomes quite real to us. These feasts really are "appointments" — appointments not just with God, but appointments with Jesus. **The Jewish Feasts are Jesus Feasts!**

---

[a] Rooftops in this region are traditionally flat which enables the homeowners to utilize their roofs for various purposes.

SUMMARY OF FEASTS

Pesach (Nisan 14)	Passover CRUCIFIXION	Each family sacrifices one lamb in remembrance of their rescue from bondage in Egypt. This feast was fulfilled by the sacrifice of JESUS CHRIST.
Hag-Ha-Matzot (Nisan 15)	Unleavened Bread PURGING SIN	All leaven is taken from the home during this week-long feast. The penalty of sin (represented by leaven) was taken from mankind and placed on JESUS CHRIST.
Bikkurim (Sun. after Sat. after Passover)	Firstfruits RESURRECTION	A sheaf of grain from the first yearly harvest is offered to the Lord. On Easter morning came the discovery of the first one ever to be resurrected from the dead, JESUS CHRIST.
Shavout (50 days after Firstfruits)	Feast of Weeks PENTECOST	Another harvest sacrifice offered to the Lord was two loaves baked with leaven. The promised Holy Spirit came and indwelt believers (both Jewish and Gentile). This combined group is called the Church or body of JESUS CHRIST.
— (Four month gap) — Rosh HaShanah (Tishri 1)	Trumpets RAPTURE	A day of judgment and gathering which was announced by an all-day blowing of trumpets. The hope of all believers is the Rapture when they will be taken up into heaven by none other than JESUS CHRIST.
Yom Kippur (Tishri 15)	Atonement Day SECOND COMING	On this solemn day the high priest offered a sacrifice for the sins of the nation. A one-time sacrifice for all mankind was made by the High Priest, JESUS CHRIST.
Succoth (Tishri 15)	Tabernacles MILLENNIUM	This festive celebration commemorated God's provision in the past and His promised Messianic Kingdom of the future. The coming Millennium of peace will be ruled over by the coming King, JESUS CHRIST.

✿ ✿ ✿ ✿ ✿ ✿

SECTION IV
FESTIVALS WITH HIDDEN TRUTH

After examining first-century, Jewish marriage customs and the feasts mandated to Israel, we must take pause. We observed that in each of the seven feasts as well as in marriage, God painted a prophetic picture of redemption. As summarized, those feasts are "appointments with Jesus."

The two additional celebrations in this section must be held up to a bright light to see their prophetic pictures. At first these canvases will appear blank. Look closely with me. The attributes of God hidden in these celebrations will send us to our knees with awe. In preparation to explore these new festivals, let us review the attributes we will discover.

The Almighty, Most Holy God, is indisputably a God of both love and faithfulness. God created us with free will, but He knew this gift would also be the instrument of our undoing. He understood that our ability to make choices would lead each of us along a stumbling pilgrimage to answer the question, "Who will be God in my life?"

We all begin our journey of life by succumbing to the tempter's ancient lie, "You can be God." This self-centeredness begins at an early age as we exhibit the desire to control our own life and environment. For a time, we struggle to live out this lie of "godhood." Eventually, we discover our inability to perform this role.

We fail because it is our nature. Our humanity dooms us to failure.[a]

When we recognize this inability, our reaction to God's loving plan of rescue becomes vital. With our free will, we have the option of falling on our knees before our Creator, or continuing the hopeless struggle to be "god" of our life. If we choose to worship God Almighty, He, in His divine providence, has made certain that our repentant heart will understand the salvation which He lovingly designed for us.[b]

Unfortunately, when faced with the need for God, many deny this need. These return to the tempter, Satan, and in essence say, "Tell me again how I can be God. I love the idea of possessing all wisdom. Tell me how I can design my own religion."[c]

This struggle for godship is subtly demonstrated for us in two special days of commemoration which have great significance in the hearts of Jewish people. These two celebrations reveal a different spiritual side of Israel than do the feasts. The wedding ceremony and the seven feasts mandated by God show us great spiritual heights and hope, but the two added celebrations illustrate a time of

---

[a] The theological term for this bent toward spiritual failure is called a "sin nature." God expresses this truth in many ways but nowhere more clearly than in these words. *"There is none righteous, no, not one."* He also states that we *"were by nature the children of wrath."* Romans 3:10; Ephesians 2:3

[b] The Bible promises, *"He that seeketh findeth"* (Matthew 7:8), yet it also states, *"There is none that seeketh after God."*(Romans 3:11). God's Word in I John 4:19 beautifully combines these two truths. *"We love him, because he first loved us."*

[c] These prideful expressions were first spoken to God by Lucifer as recorded in Isaiah 14:13, 14. Lucifer (Satan) then tempted humankind with the same "godship" principle when he said, *"In the day ye eat thereof, then your eyes shall be opened, and ye shall be as gods."* Genesis 3:5. Cain continued this lie by designing a works-centered religion. Genesis 4:1-15

despair and apostasy. Still, in the midst of this sadness there is hope—hope not just in the faith evidenced by a small remnant of people but an even larger hope. We see hope in a great God who remains faithful even when His children turn their backs on Him.

CHAPTER 10
PURIM

A tiny historical book containing only ten chapters lies nestled in the pages of the Old Testament Scriptures. Seldom do Christian pastors even refer to its contents, yet within Judaism this book receives great attention. Its chronicle of royal romance, intrigue, murderous scheming, bravery, and rescue have produced an annual day of celebration like no other on the Jewish calendar. The book is Esther and the festival is Purim.

To understand the deep significance of Purim, we must understand the story recounted in Esther. But to understand Esther, we must go back to the beginning, to the very beginning, when God made man. Only then will we gain true understanding of this unique celebration and its significance to all humanity.

Very early in humankind's existence, God gave a promise. He prophesied that one day a woman would give birth to a Savior who would crush Satan.[a] This promise of a Savior who would defeat Satan brought great hope to humanity—understandably this message was not received with enthusiasm by Satan.

---

[a] Genesis 3:15

Sprinkled throughout the rest of the Bible we read of countless attempts by Satan to thwart God's pronouncement of doom. Satan's strategy was clear. He must eliminate any women who God might use to deliver the Savior. If that plan failed, he would withdraw to his second line of defense and simply eliminate the Savior.[a] He reasoned, "No Savior, Satan wins."

Many feel Satan's first concentrated effort was an attack against all humankind in the days of Noah. Since before the time of Christ, the belief has existed that the giants spoken of in Genesis, chapter 6, were the result of fallen angels intermarrying with humans. Many believe these satanically-nurtured liaisons were an attempt to infiltrate and pollute the human race, thus making it impossible for any woman to be a fit vessel to give birth to the Messiah.[b]

Although theologians disagree on whether or not this intermingling occurred, enough good scholars support the idea to give it consideration. Arno C. Gaebelein states, "These evil beings came down out of the air and began to take possession of the daughters of men as they chose."[97c]

Among many proofs for this bizarre mix, they point to God's statement in Genesis 6:9; "*Noah was a just man and*

---

[a] As outlined in Passover, Satan actually thought he had eliminated the Savior by instigating the death of Christ. He failed, however, to fathom the spiritual nature of the Crucifixion nor did he understand that Jesus would conquer death.

[b] If indeed this was a satanic strategy, there may have been other similar attempts to pollute the wombs of specific women in the promised line of Christ. This possibility is seen in the lives of Sarah and Rebekah (Genesis 12:10-18; 20:1-9; 26:6-10).

[c] Stanley Price lists scores of sources that agree with this premise. Among others he names Philo, Josephus, most of the rabbis, the Septuagint, Kurtz, Delitzsch, Gunkel, Konigand, Pember, Milton, Gray and Jennings. (See Bibliography, Price Stanley. *The Giants of Noah's Day.*)

perfect in his generations." They believe God informs us in this passage that Noah and his ancestors had not yet succumbed to the alluring temptation of demonic love-making.

If indeed this was Satan's plan to terminate the possibility of a Savior coming, he obviously underestimated God. Most people refer to the Flood as a story of destruction. It is. But even more, it is a story of divine love and rescue. Whether the rescue was from physical as well as spiritual pollution, God saved the human race.

After this and every other futile Satanic attempt to abort God's Word, you can almost imagine Satan pulling a black cape over his face and saying, "Curses foiled again!"

After the Flood, God spoke directly to a man known as Abraham. God told him to leave the country of his birth and go to a new land. There, God prophesied, Abraham would become the father of a great nation. God also guaranteed this new Promised Land would belong to Abraham and his *"seed for ever."*[a] The blessings of this land would flow freely as long as his descendants remained in the land and obeyed God.[b]

Another pivotal promise made to Abraham was, *"In thee shall all families of the earth be blessed."*[c] This prophecy, later verified to Isaac and Jacob, Abraham's descendants,[d] signified that the promised Savior would come from their lineage.

---

[a] Genesis 13:15

[b] Deuteronomy, chapters 28-30

[c] Genesis 12:3

[d] Known today as Jews (see Genesis 28:13-15)

As soon as Satan heard the details about this specific lineage of the Savior, he concentrated his further attacks on Abraham and the Jewish nation. He knew that if he could eliminate the Jews altogether, he would be victorious over God. If he could prove God to be ineffectual at keeping His promise, Satan's sentence of doom would be neutralized.

We must remember that Satan's ultimate goal has always been to replace God. Satan desires to reign as master of the universe. His method to achieve this status is to eliminate the chosen nation of Israel in order to depict God as incompetent.[a] Throughout history there have been attempts that demonstrate this on-going, murderous bent of Satan.

Noted Bible teacher, Arthur Pink, reminds us of some biblically chronicled attacks of Satan. "The 'famines' mentioned in Genesis were the first efforts of the enemy to destroy the fathers of the chosen race. The edict of Pharaoh to destroy all the male children; the Egyptian attack at the Red Sea; the assaults of the Canaanites when in the land, the plot of Haman are all examples of the enmity between Satan and the 'woman'."[98]

The "plot of Haman" mentioned here comes directly from the book of Esther. This special book records yet another foiled attempt of Satan to literally erase the Jewish nation.

From the Exodus to the time of Esther, the Jewish nation experienced many highs and lows. For the first five hundred years under the leadership of judges, there were times of both obedience and apostasy. Around 1095 B.C.,

---

[a] God stakes His own reputation on His ability to preserve the Jewish nation. In Jeremiah 31:35-37 God promises that His ability to preserve Israel is more dependable than the purposes of the sun, moon, stars, and oceans.

God allowed Israel to have kings who would rule over their country. Under the first three kings (Saul, David and Solomon), Israel reached its zenith in size and prosperity.[a] Most importantly they worshipped God.

However, life changed after Solomon's death. Civil war split the kingdom of Israel in half and an ever-accelerating, downward spiral of apostasy began. After repeated warnings to Israel to repent and return to godly living, God allowed foreign nations to overrun Israel, capture and take the Jews out of the Promised Land.

God even foretold the exact length of the time the Jews would be captives. *"This whole land shall be a desolation, and an astonishment; and these nations shall serve the king of Babylon seventy years."*[b] After the Jews were freed from bondage in Egypt, God forewarned them about another potential ordeal of captivity. He said if the Jews failed to let the land lie fallow one year out of every seven, they would eventually have to pay back those years by being captives in a heathen land.[c] In essence, God would force the Jews out so the land could rest. By 605 B.C., they had allowed 490 years to pass without allowing the land to rest, so they owed seventy years.

In 536 B.C., after paying back **exactly** seventy years, the captivity ended. In a dramatic move, God touched the

---

[a] Never in the history of Israel have the Jews occupied all of the land God gave them. Under David and Solomon, they possessed only 30,000 square miles of the 300,000 promised to them. See Deuteronomy 11:23-25.

[b] Jeremiah 25:1-14. As well as the length of captivity, this passage also explains the reason for the capture. Compare also II Chronicles 36:21-23

[c] Leviticus 26:32-35, 43

heart of Cyrus, King of Persia,[a] causing him to release all the Jewish captives. This act wonderfully demonstrates the providential hand of God. Conquering monarchs were not in the habit of letting enslaved people return to their homes!

Unbelievably, out of the two million Jews living in captivity, less than sixty thousand returned. Why didn't they rush home? Very simply as Ezra and Nehemiah record, the rebuilding of Jerusalem was an arduous task. After seventy years in a foreign culture, most of the Jews had grown soft; they no longer objected to the heathen practices of Persia. They simply had no desire to deny themselves comfort, return to their land of promise, and resume the worship of God as He had instructed. (Today, believers in Jesus also struggle with this tendency of choosing self-comfort instead of obedience to God.)

The Book of Esther

Finally we come to Esther. First, the uniqueness of this book must be addressed. Study the ten chapters. Search the pages. **You'll not find one mention of God in this book.** There is also no mention of prayer or worship, yet we see God in control, orchestrating people and events, making certain that He protects His chosen people. We call these occurrences the providence of God.[b]

---

[a] The Babylonian Empire, which had originally taken the Jews captive, had subsequently been overrun by the Persian Empire.

[b] God had demonstrated His providence many times before. For example, He made sure that the Pharaoh's daughter would see the basket floating in the Nile River and that the baby would cry just as she saw the child so that her heart would melt and Moses would be spared.

When relating providence to the story of Esther, J. Vernon McGee contributes one of his typically homey but accurate definitions. "Providence is the way God leads the man who will not be led."[99]

Rabbi Elkanah Schwartz gives us a unique description of the reason for Purim that fits well into the book of Esther. "The reason—to remind us of that important aspect of our faith: the 'Hidden Face' of the Almighty, which functions not only on Purim, but eternally."[100] This rabbi, too, sees God behind the scenes in Esther.

Xerxes the Great ruled the mighty Persian Empire from the palace at Shushan.[a] For both political and social purposes, Xerxes organized the most lavish banquet the world has ever seen. Several thousand of his princely cabinet (from the one hundred and twenty-seven provinces throughout the fertile crescent[b]) attended his opulent affair. Not only did he offer the finest in food and entertainment, the gala lasted **six months.**

At the end of a seven-day grand finale, Xerxes and the rest of the merrymakers were decidedly drunk. Against all proprieties of the day, he called assistants to bring in one more trophy. He summoned Vashti, his beautiful queen, intending to show her off to the drunken guests. She refused to come.

---

[a] The great city of Shushan (Susa) lay at the southern end of the royal Persian road. A map today would show the city to be in Iran about fifty miles northeast of Kuwait and fifty miles east of Iraq.

In Esther, Ahasuerus is named as the king in the text, but this is a title like Caesar. History shows us Xerxes is the king described in Esther.

[b] His empire spread between the Southern borders from India to Ethiopia and Northern borders from Turkey to Kazakhstan. The purpose of this affair was to impress his leaders with the wealth and might of his empire in order to convince them to go to war against Greece. Xerxes wanted to rule all of the known world.

Of course, not only the king but the rest of the men quickly sobered. They realized that if this queen could successfully disobey her husband, then the wives of the delegates (and the rest of the women in the kingdom as well) might follow her example. Xerxes wisely banished Vashti and organized a beauty pageant to find a new, more cooperative queen.

In this heathen land, at a debauched celebration, in the heart of a pagan king, God was in control. We will recognize the outcome of this banquet as divine providence.

Persia, like most countries throughout history, was anti-Semitic. The Jews who lived successfully in this community hid their Jewish heritage. Mordecai was no exception. He worked in the palace. A kind man, he also had raised Esther, his young orphaned cousin, as his own daughter. Since she possessed great beauty, he entered her in the national, royal, year-long, beauty contest organized to find a new queen.

Entering that contest at first sounds like a wise decision, but what had **God said** about intermarriage with the heathen? *"Ye shall not go in to them."*[a] Nehemiah called intermarriage with pagans *"a great evil"* and a transgression *"against our God."*[b]

We must come to grips here with a vital truth. The Jews (Mordecai and Esther) who are key players in this story are out of the will of God. No matter how honorable, how brave or how significant their actions turn out to be, they are living in disobedience to God. Not only were these two conspiring together to have Esther marry a

---

[a] I Kings 11:1, 2

[b] Nehemiah 13:27

non-believer, they (and the other two million Jews in Persia) did not even belong in that land. God had repeatedly told His chosen people to stay in the Promised Land of Israel. Although the Jews had originally come to this heathen country as captives, they were now free to go back to Israel. But they stayed.

Now God was compelled by His love and commitment to His chosen people to provide for their survival in a hostile environment. Remember also that Satan was constantly at work behind the scenes. He continued to look for some method to annihilate God's people.

As the story unfolds, Xerxes looks at Esther and instantly becomes smitten with her beauty. King Xerxes loved Esther, but still she did not reveal her Jewishness to her new husband. (Sadly, Mordecai had risked Esther's total future in this contest since the losers in the contest automatically became part of the Persian king's sizable harem!)

Another character enters the story whose name is Haman. His lineage as an Agagite casts him as a bad actor, and as the new prime minister of Persia, he is in position to do great harm. (Agagites originated five hundred years before, after King Saul had directly disobeyed God by sparing the life of King Agag. Saul actually lost his kingship because of his rebellious omission which God likened to the sin of witchcraft.)[a]

Haman demonstrated the evil characteristics of his lineage. He plotted the mass murder of every Jew in the Persian Empire (which would have included the faithful remnant in Israel). All this murderous anger rose up in Haman because of his wounded pride. You see, Mordecai had refused to bow when Haman passed by. Haman

---

[a] I Samuel 15:23

inquired about this insolent underling, and when he found out Mordecai was a Jew, Haman's satanically inspired anti-Semitism ignited.

King Xerxes believed the lies Haman concocted about the Jews and gave approval to the scheme of annihilation. Haman gathered the court magicians together in the first month (Nisan) for the purpose of casting lots to determine the best day to carry out this nefarious deed. The lot casting, called pur, fell on the thirteenth day of the twelfth month (Adar).

David C. Gross, a Jewish scholar, gives us great insight into the celebration of Purim. "The fourteenth of Adar coincided with a holiday period in the pagan calendar in western Asia.[a] Haman may deliberately have chosen a holiday of this sort for the execution of his plans.[b] The merrymaking, half-inebriated rabble could more easily be aroused to join in the slaughter of innocent people, especially if the latter were unprotected by the authorities and if loot were in prospect."[101]

Satan, thinking he was in charge, no doubt selected this evil day for the massacre by manipulating the cast lots, but God even controlled the occultic, divining tools of the magicians. God provided a full year from the casting of lots until the murdering was to be done (which gave time for the plan to be discovered and overridden.)

Esther braved possible death by approaching the king without being summoned. He granted audience to Esther

---

[a] History shows that this pagan holiday appears to have been the lewd festival of the Spring Equinox (found on the **Satanic Ritual Calendar**). Most cultures celebrated this as a time of bringing some deity back from the dead as well as fertility adoration. The day's vile "sacredness" defies reason.

[b] For accuracy we must note that the Bible says "the casting of lots" not Haman selected the day.

and listened to her story. During several days of banqueting and intrigue she revealed details to the king about the treachery of Haman, the faithfulness of Mordecai, and her own Jewishness.

Xerxes loved Esther and desired to solve the dilemma but a logistical problem existed. Xerxes ruled an empire, not just a small country where communication was rapid and everyone spoke the same language. Remember, the vast Persian Empire encompassed one hundred and twenty-seven provinces. Previous dispatches had gone out in the first month of the year mandating that on the thirteenth day of the twelfth month all Jews were to be killed and their possessions taken. It would take time to reach everyone with a new message.

Even more difficult to overcome was the fact that King Xerxes could not break his own proclamation! The Bible explains, *"The law of the Medes and the Persians is, That no decree nor statute which the king establisheth may be changed."*[a] But Xerxes solved the impossible problem. He wrote a **new law** granting *"the Jews which were in every city to gather themselves together, and to stand for their life, to destroy, to slay, and to cause to perish, all the power of the people and province that would assault them."*[b]

This new decree went out, delivered by messengers riding mules and camels. Of course the Jews of the Persian Empire were delighted. They now had permission from the king to organize and destroy the exponents of anti-Semitism. On this Jewish calendar day of Nisan the 17th, the decree went out that saved the Jews from

---

[a] Daniel 6:15

[b] Esther 8:11

extinction. Also on this day, the satanically inspired Haman was executed.

Here again we see the providence of God, as he preserved His chosen people. In a single day He saved the nation. But notice, He also ordained that the rescue and the execution of their would-be murderer was on **the exact day of the Feast of Firstfruits, God's prophetic day of rescue!**[a]

Nine months later, the date of Adar the thirteenth arrived (which was the date originally selected by Haman for all the Jews to be annihilated). On this day instead, the would-be killers of the Jews lost more than seventy thousand of their members to the sword.

Since the lot (pur) had fallen on the thirteenth of Adar[b], selecting it as the day of massacre, the fourteenth was chosen as the day of celebration. The Bible records, "*The Jews that were at Shushan assembled together on the thirteenth day thereof, and on the fourteenth thereof; and on the fifteenth day of the same they rested, and made it a day of feasting and gladness...and a good day, and of sending portions one to another...Wherefore they called these days Purim after the name of Pur.*"[c]

After this unbelievable rescue from certain destruction we would expect some thanks, at least token thanks to God. But no. We see celebration. We see gift giving and we even see a national day of commemoration established, but sadly, no recognition that God in His providence had saved His people.

---

[a] Resurrection Day (See earlier chapter on Firstfruits.)

[b] This Jewish calendar date occurs in February or March. Purim is always thirty days before Passover.

[c] Esther 9:18, 19, 26

Purim Today

Although the commemoration of Purim can be traced back to its time and place of origin, the ceremonies and festivities as they are seen today were not formalized until the third century A.D. During this extended, joyous celebration, the story of Esther is read on Purim Eve. The rabbis spit as the name of Haman is mentioned. They say, "'Let his name be blotted out,' or 'Let him be accursed'."[102]

In actuality, most of the festivities of Purim resemble paganism more than giving thanks to God. Children wear costumes. Some dress up like Esther or other characters in the account so they can reenact the story. Mostly, though, today as you walk the streets of Israel, you will see children dressed as ghosts, goblins, Ninja turtles, or monsters. The decorations in the stores and homes remind observers of the pagan Halloween decorations found in the United States.

Curiously, this is the one time of the year that people are encouraged to drink liquor until intoxicated. According to Rabbi Elkanah Schwartz, "The rabbis say: 'a person is enjoined to drink on Purim till he no longer knows the difference between the words, 'cursed be Haman' and 'blessed be Mordecai'."[103]

Today, as one observes the celebration of Purim in Israel, the question does come to mind, "What does this dressing in bizarre, pagan costumes, exchanging gifts, and frantic merrymaking and drinking have to do with the awesome rescue of the nation of Israel?"

Hidden Truths of Purim

Although the thankless attitude in Esther is reprehensible, it is but a mirror image of humanity. As stated in the introduction to Purim, everyone has a lifelong struggle with the question, "Who will be God in my life?" We must also ask, "Who will we look to for help and guidance? Who will we thank for our rescue?" Just as Esther, Mordecai, and the rest of the Jews in Persia failed to give God glory, so we all struggle with this issue on a daily basis. I am afraid that every reader of these words, including myself, can recall similar instances of misplaced godship and thanklessness in our own lives.

What then are the "hidden truths" found, both leading up to and in the festival of Purim? There are many. In brief we will review ten.

1) **The land of Israel is sacred.** It is God's. God calls Israel *"The land which ye shall inhabit, wherein I dwell."* He proclaims, *"The land is mine."*[a] The world is beginning to focus on the tiny piece of land called Israel. People of many religions and political persuasions would do well to recognize that first and foremost, Israel is sacred ground.

2) **The Jews are God's chosen people.** *"O Israel...I have called thee by thy name; thou art mine."* He will preserve them. *"Know therefore that the Lord thy God, he is God, the faithful God, which keepeth covenant and mercy with them that love him and keep his commandments to a thousand generations."*[b]

3) **God gave the land of Israel to the Jews forever.** *"I will establish my covenant between me and thee and thy seed after thee in their generations for an everlasting covenant...I will give unto thee, and to thy seed after thee, the land wherein thou art a stranger, all the land of Canaan, for an everlasting*

---

[a] Numbers 35:34; Leviticus 25:23

[b] Isaiah 43:1; Deuteronomy 7:9

possession." It is the place of blessing for the nation of Israel. *"The Lord your God hath given you rest, and hath given you this land."* [a]

4) **The Jews would be taken from the land for disobedience.** *"If thou wilt not hearken unto the voice of the Lord thy God, to observe to do all his commandments and his statutes which I command thee this day; that all these curses shall come upon thee, and overtake thee...and ye shall be plucked from off the land."* God foretold that expulsion would occur. *"This people will rise up...and will forsake me, and break my covenant which I have made with them."* [b]

5) **Banishment would not last forever.** *"For a small moment have I forsaken thee; but with great mercies will I gather thee."* God is faithful to His promises. *"For the mountains shall depart, and the hills be removed; but my kindness shall not depart from thee, neither shall the covenant of my peace be removed, saith the Lord."* God expressed the tenderness of His love toward His people even when they had ignored Him. *"Can a woman forget her suckling child, that she should not have compassion on the son of her womb? yea, they may forget, yet will I not forget thee. Behold, I have graven thee upon the palms of my hands."* [c]

6) **Thanklessness always has broken God's heart.** Psalm 107, contains four stanzas which describe dramatic accounts of God's rescue. After each stanza we hear these

---

[a] Genesis 17:7, 8; Joshua 1:13; Deuteronomy 28:1-14

[b] Deuteronomy 28:15, 63; (for more details see Deuteronomy 28:15-68; 29:24-28); Deuteronomy 31:16

[c] Isaiah 54:7, 10; 49:15-16 (See also the beautiful promises of Leviticus 26:44; Psalm 89:26-34, and Romans, chapters 9-11)

poignant words from God. *"Oh that men would praise the Lord for his goodness, and for his wonderful works to the children of men!"*[a]

7) **Apathy promotes destruction.** In an effort to live comfortably and avoid the demands connected with returning to their homeland, the Jews effectively declined divine protection. This apathy nearly cost the nation of Israel their life! Were it not for the faithfulness of God, there would be no Jews today. Neither Jews then, nor Christians today, can expect the blessings of God when at the same time they are blending with the world. If we hide our identification with God, He will not even hear our prayers. *"He that turneth away his ear from hearing the law, even his prayer shall be abomination." "If I regard iniquity in my heart, the Lord will not hear me." "Wherefore come out from among them, and be ye separate, saith the Lord."*[b]

8) **The decrees of Xerxes picture sin and salvation.** Nothing appears on the pages of the Bible by accident. Another "hidden truth" surfaces in the two laws mandated by Xerxes. First, we see a decree to kill every Jew. Then Xerxes designs a second decree that potentially could override the first law. I say potentially because if the Jews failed to take the threat of death seriously, if they failed to respond, they would still be killed. Remember, even though he was king, Xerxes could not annul his own decree.

God has decreed death upon all humankind as the penalty for sin. *"The soul that sinneth, it shall die."* That decree is still in effect. The justice of God cannot be left

---

[a] Psalm 107:1-31

[b] Proverbs 28:9; Psalm 66:18; II Corinthians 6:17

unsatisfied. God's second decree describes the work of Jesus on the cross. *"Having forgiven you all trespasses; Blotting out the handwriting of ordinances that was against us, which was contrary to us, and took it out of the way, nailing it to his cross."* In this next verse the two "decrees" of God are summed up. *"The wages of sin is death; but the gift of God is eternal life through Jesus Christ our Lord."*[a]

9) **God won new converts in spite of the poor witness of His people.** God is amazing. Even when the Jews hid their identification with God, the message of God's power still became known. After the second decree went out and the Jews began to celebrate and feast openly, many people converted to Judaism.

Some people object to preaching a gospel of "fear," yet Esther and other biblical accounts display examples of people converting to God from fear. The testimony of Rahab is one such example. *"We have heard how the Lord dried up the water of the Red Sea for you, when ye came out of Egypt; and what ye did unto the two kings of the Amorites...whom ye utterly destroyed. And as soon as we had heard these things, our hearts did melt, neither did there remain any more courage in any man, because of you: for the Lord your God, he is God in heaven above, and in earth beneath."* Remember, the Bible says, *"The fear of the Lord is the beginning of knowledge."*[b]

Only a few in Rahab's day who heard were converted, but in Esther's time *"Many of the people of the land became*

---

[a] Ezekiel 18:4; Colossians 2:13, 14; Romans 6:23

[b] Joshua 2:10, 11; Proverbs 1:7

Jews; for the fear of the Jews fell upon them."[a] We may have been hiding our belief in Jesus but when (if) we allow those around us to see the power of God in our lives, they too may become believers.

10) **Satan continues to attack God's people.** The Holocaust reveals Satan's handiwork. This twentieth century tragedy in Germany certainly substantiates Satan's current activities. He continues to pursue his intention of eliminating every one of God's chosen people, the Jews. Even within Islam, we see his work in the denial of Israel's right to exist.

The evil thread of Satan's intentions is even seen in the activities of the United Nations. Apart from recognizing Satan's manipulations behind the scenes in the political realm, one cannot logically explain why **more than half of all U.N. resolutions** since the inception of the state of Israel in 1948 have been against one tiny nation, Israel. With all the genocide and ruthless governments worldwide, why does Israel receive all the criticism? We find the answer in Satan who "*as a roaring lion, walketh about, seeking whom he may devour.*"[b] He will continue to stalk his prey (Israel) even into the seven years of Tribulation. "*The dragon was wroth with the woman, and went to make war with the remnant of her seed.*"[c] Praise God! Israel is one morsel Satan will never devour.

---

[a] Esther 8:17

[b] I Peter 5:8

[c] Revelation 12:17

REVIEW OF PURIM

In the twenty-five hundred years since Esther, the attacks of Satan against the Jews have continued almost unabated. Were it not for the continued providential care of God, Satan would have succeeded. Numerous countries, as well as individual despots, carried out these satanic acts of genocide, but God was always in control. God's Word declares, *"The king's heart is in the hand of the Lord, as the rivers of water: he turneth it whithersoever he will."* and *"Behold, he that keepeth Israel shall neither slumber nor sleep."*[a]

Remember though, until 1948, the nation of Israel was still in dispersion. God still had them under the providence of His disciplining hand. After gaining statehood in 1948, the situation changed politically for the Jews, but what about the spiritual climate? The providential hand of God is clearly recognized in the military victories, yet listen to the tales of victory. Do we hear acknowledgments of gratitude toward God or do we hear echoes of Esther? Some acknowledge the source of their triumphs as divine. Most do not. The cry today is still for a Messiah to come and bring peace; they are not yet seeking a Messiah to cover sins.

Bigger than the battle against neighbors who pursue Israel's destruction is the battle within the heart of each person. The oldest battle continues over "To whom will I bow down, myself or God?"

The same loving God that taught, chastised, remained faithful, and rescued His chosen people, the Jews, has a message for Christians today. After reviewing Old Testament examples of Jewish struggles, God counsels us,

---

[a] Proverbs 21:1; Psalm 121:4

"Now all these things happened to them for examples: and are written for our admonition."[a]

Even though God's name is not mentioned in Esther, by looking closely, we see His hand. How beautifully appropriate is the Jewish idiom for Purim, the "Hidden God."

Will Purim be used on God's prophetic calendar or is it just recorded for our remembrance and exhortation? Time will reveal the answer. For now, Purim and the history of God's love leading up to it fill us with awesome respect for our Lord.

---

[a] I Corinthians 10:11

CHAPTER 11
HANUKKAH

Every year, as Christians prepare for the observance of Christmas, Traditional and Orthodox Jews plan for the celebration of Hanukkah. Is this celebration day simply an alternative holiday for Jews or does it have deeper roots? If this is a religious day, what "hidden truths" might it hold for Christians?

The Hebrew name of this feast, Hanukkah, means "dedication." This festival commemorates a Jewish victory led by Judas Maccabeas[a] during the early second century B.C. Neither the Jewish Bible nor the Protestant Old Testament contain the account of this victory since the latest book included in both is Malachi, penned in 397 B.C. However, the historical books of Maccabees, found in the Catholic Bible, chronicle this account as does Josephus the great historian of the first century A.D.

Most people outside of Judaism are only vaguely aware of today's eight-day Hanukkah ceremony. Modern Jews celebrate with greeting cards, giving small sums of money to children and exchanging of gifts much like the traditions of Christmas.

---

[a] The family name (plural) is spelled "Maccabees"

A special eight-cup candle holder gains the center of attention during an extended ceremony of candle lighting.[a] The observance begins on the eve of Kislev 24,[b] by the kindling of the first light in each home. The candles (or cups of oil) must stay lit for at least one-half hour before being extinguished. On each successive day of the eight, another light is added, until on the last day all eight are lit.

As in all the other Jewish commemorative days, scores of intricate rules and details must be observed. The type of oil, the length of candle, the placement of the candlestick, activities that may be done in the glow of these lights, who must be present, and many more requirements are woven throughout this special ceremony.

The service connected with the lights includes reciting prayers about miracles and thanksgiving, as well as the Hallel prayers of Psalms 113-118. Scriptures from Exodus 40, Psalms, the whole books of Zechariah and I Kings are read. Various other readings take place including some from Judith and Maccabees. Singing includes the song "Moaz Tzur," which means "O Fortress, the Rock of My Salvation."

Another popular name for this holiday is Hag Haorim, or the "Festival of Lights." The custom of the lighting of candles is based on the story of oil being miraculously supplied when Judas Maccabeas cleansed the Temple in 165 B.C. Since the best histories of the cleansing found in Josephus and Maccabees don't even mention the "miracle of the oil," it appears to be a legend formed after the first century, A.D.

---

[a] This lampstand or candleholder, the Hanukkaiyyah, is not the same as the familiar seven-branched Menorah we see as the national symbol of Israel.

[b] This Jewish month and day falls somewhere between late November and late December.

Although this festival is not ordained by God in the Old Testament, there are three areas we can explore to find its hidden truth:

1) the historical/religious importance as it relates to the Jews,
2) the New Testament celebration of Hanukkah, and
3) its prophetic impact as revealed in the book of Daniel.

The Historical/Religious Importance

First, we must do a short historical review of the land of Israel. The Middle East has been the focus of land battles since creation. Always in the center of these battles is the area known as Israel. The following list includes only some of the people-groups who have fought for (and for awhile claimed) ownership of Israel: 1) Canaanites, 2) Israelites, 3) Ethiopians, 4) Assyrians, 5) Babylonians, 6) Medes, 7) Persians, 8) Greeks, 9) Romans, 10) Abbasids, 11) Sassanids, 12) Omayyads, 13) Fatimites, 14) Seljuk Turks, 15) Ayyubids, 16) Ottomans, 17) British, and 18) Jews/Palestinians. The preserving providence of God is seen by the disappearance of many of these people-groups. They no longer exist, yet the Jews, even without autonomy, live on.

Although lust for power and greed continues producing wars around the globe, **no area has been conquered and lost as often as has Israel.** One might explain, "That area is close to the cradle of civilization[a] so, of course, it has seen more war. It has seen more people."

Yes, that is somewhat true. But better reason is needed to explain the centuries of confrontation in this area. Consider the countless wars over the ownership of Jerusalem. This Middle East conflict has been a religious war almost from the beginning. There is reason to believe this struggle for control emanates in the spirit realm.

God is a Spirit and not confined to any one geographical location but He does maintain a location in heaven. Apparently God's throne in heaven is where His created beings can come to worship Him.[b] God also claims a particular location on the earth which is Israel, and more specifically, the city of Jerusalem. Even more precisely, He claims the site of Solomon's Temple by announcing, I have *"chosen this place to myself for a house of sacrifice...mine eyes and mine heart shall be there perpetually."*[c]

Satan is a usurper, desiring to be God. Sometime in eternity-past he actually boasted, "*I will be like God.*" That lust for godship also prompts him to battle for God's property. Satan bragged, "*I will ascend into heaven, I will exalt my throne above the stars of God.*"[d]

Unbelievably, the same pride that prompted Satan's attempt to be "god" in eternity-past also nourishes his delusion that he is winning his war against God.

---

[a] The area along the Euphrates river in Iraq where the Garden of Eden is thought to have been. Even sociologists believe this is where the civilization of "early" man began.

[b] Revelation 4:1-11

[c] II Chronicles 7:12, 16

[d] Isaiah 14:12-17

Sometimes, Satan appears to gain the upper hand in this property dispute, but those who believe the Bible can see Satan's twisted use of statistics.

Satan uses the **quantity** of people who follow him to prove his expertise; God demonstrates His power by the **quality** He produces in people's lives. Satan can only destroy his followers; God brings life. In referring to Satan, Jesus teaches, "*The thief cometh not, but for to steal, and to kill, and to destroy: I am come that they might have life, and that they might have it more abundantly.*"[a]

Satan cannot be omnipresent as is God. This deceiver must have a geographical headquarters from which to control his "*principalities*" and "*powers*" and "*rulers of darkness.*"[b] The last location listed in the Bible for Satan's throne was Pergamos, a city in Turkey.[c] Is he still headquartered there? Perhaps. It certainly provides an ideal lookout post over Jerusalem, the city he wants so badly to occupy.

The Origin of Hanukkah

Hanukkah dates back to the second century B.C. To understand Hanukkah, and the "hidden information" it contains, we need to examine the life of an evil man central to the story. The deeds of this man prepicture events yet to occur in God's prophetic plan. In order to get the full impact of this evil man's place on the stage of

---

[a] John 10:10

[b] Ephesians 6:12

[c] Revelation 2:13, 14

history, we must go back some one hundred and fifty years **before** he came to power.

****

In 323 B.C., Alexander the Great ruled over the Grecian Empire. His middle eastern armies controlled boundaries quite similar to those of the Persian Empire of Xerxes the Great. Actually, the arrogant, military advance Xerxes had presented at his lavish banquet (described in the book of Esther) failed completely. His attempt to conquer all the world in 480 B.C. floundered when he challenged superior forces in Greece; his empire never fully recovered. In 332 B.C., the Persian world succumbed to the military genius of Alexander the Great of Greece. The entire Persian Empire fell to Alexander.

Unfortunately, Alexander fueled his brain with alcohol causing his death at age thirty-three. Just as prophesied in the book of Daniel, the Grecian Empire was broken up and divided among four generals.[a] One of the four divisions of the empire was the eastern section of the empire including Syria, which was taken over by Seleucus Nicator; another was Egypt and North Africa which became the domain of Ptolemy. These two generals (now turned kings) and their heirs fought constantly. Murders occurred within families to gain power. Arrangements of political marriages between these two kingdoms took place in an effort to

---

[a] Daniel 7:6; 8:8. Specifically described in Daniel is the dividing of the Grecian Empire into four parts. Amazingly, the empires of Babylon, Persia, Greece, and Rome are all prophesied in Daniel. See chapters 2, 7, 8

gain the upper hand.[a] Always Israel seemed to be in the
middle of their battles!

A comparison of the secular history of this era with the
precise prophesies in Daniel, chapter 11, reveal amazing
fulfillments. This discovery brings us once more to our
knees in awe. Jehovah God knows the future. He is in
control.

The Bible gives detailed prophesies about the leaders
who took over the four divisions of the Grecian Empire.
The book of Daniel (written in 534 B.C.) contains specific,
prophetic information about a *"vile person"* to come. Daniel
describes that coming leader as a successor to the throne of
the Syrian segment of the old Grecian Empire.

He *"shall come in peaceably, and obtain the kingdom by
flatteries."* He will overthrow *"the prince of the covenant,"*
speak *"lies"* at negotiation tables, and lead a successful
campaign against Egypt. A second attack against Egypt
would fail. He would *"have indignation against the holy
covenant"* (God's laws) but *"have intelligence with them that
forsake the holy covenant."*

The vile nature of his leadership would become evident
when he commits the sacrilege described in this passage.
*"They shall pollute the sanctuary of strength, and shall take away
the daily sacrifice, and they shall place the abomination that
maketh desolate."*

Further corruption and his eventual defeat is
prophesied next. *"And such as do wickedly against the
covenant shall he corrupt by flatteries: but the people that do
know their God shall be strong, and do exploits. And they that
understand among the people shall instruct many: yet they shall*

---

[a] The most famous of these was the marriage of Cleopatra of Syria to Ptolemy
Epiphanes of Egypt. They were both twelve years old. Cleopatra's evil brother was
Antiochus Epiphanes whom we will soon discuss.

fall by the sword, and by flame, by captivity, and by spoil, many days. Now when they shall fall, they shall be helped with a little help: but many shall cleave to them with flatteries."[a]

In another passage, Daniel writes about this future, vile leader. He will move toward the *"pleasant land."*[b] Scripture also declares *"he magnified himself."* A very specific prophecy states, *"By him the daily sacrifice was taken away."* Even the length of the absence of sacrifice is described. *"Two thousand and three hundred days; then shall the sanctuary be cleansed."*[c]

Who would this vile leader be? What do these prophesies mean and did they come to pass?

The thirteen successive kings of the Syrian kingdom all carried the title of Antiochus. In 175 B.C., a new Antiochus came to the throne who all serious students of prophecy believe to be the vile person. His choice to be called Antiochus Theos Epiphanes gives insight into his devilish character. Theos Epiphanes means, "God manifest."

He came to the throne offering a program of peace. His exploits included a successful attack against Egypt and then a second one where he experienced defeat. Remember, **these exact details** had been prophesied by God and recorded by Daniel more than three hundred and fifty years earlier![d]

[a] Daniel 11:21-34

[b] This is definite reference to Israel. Jeremiah 3:19; Zechariah 7:14

[c] Daniel 8:9-14

[d] It is no wonder that God's critics become critics of the book of Daniel. Once again, fulfilled prophecy stamps the seal of divine authorship on the Bible. Satan and his henchmen hate God's ability to accurately foretell the future. Remember, Satan does not like God's outline of the future!

Epiphanes appointed a man as high priest who by God's ordinances, was unqualified. In 171 B.C. this new high priest, Menelaus, murdered Onias III, the rightful high priest. This fulfilled the prophecy of "*overthrowing the prince of the covenant.*"[a] Then, because no sanctioned high priest officiated in the Temple, the sacrifices became meaningless in God's sight. This satisfied the prophecy that "*the daily sacrifice would be taken away.*"

Throughout his reign, Epiphanes flattered, lied, and gained advantages through deceit. He was a master. Before he came to power, many unfaithful Jews had talked their peers into great apostasy. These apostates went to the new king asking for permission to follow pagan practices. They asked permission to build a gymnasium and use it as the pagans did.[b] Epiphanes authorized the project. He also seized the opportunity and, through the next few years, used these compromising turncoats as spies against their own people.

Josephus, the book of Maccabees, and some rabbis tell us that much of the anguish and killing that the Jews experienced under this evil man was due to the compromise of the Jews themselves. They were more interested in enjoying the pagan culture of the day than in serving their God; they were ripe to fall into the hands of an evil dictator. Once again, we see prophecy fulfilled. Indeed, the people of the covenant were corrupted by flatteries.

First, with the help of his Jewish spies, Epiphanes plundered Jerusalem. Then in 168 B.C., two years later, he

---

[a] Mosaic law required that the High Priest be a descendant of Levi and from the family of Aaron.

[b] The pagan practice was to strip naked for sports in the gym.

returned, pretending peace. Once inside the city, he killed forty thousand Jews, including the spies, and stole the riches of the Temple. He forbade circumcision, reading of the Torah, and he demanded that the Jews forsake all worship of Jehovah God.

For a finale, Epiphanes defiled the altar in the Temple of God. In a crushing satanic operation, he commandeered the Temple, entered the sanctuary,[a] and erected a statue of Jupiter[b] with his own face substituted on it. He also offered a pig upon the altar and spread swine blood in the Holy of Holies.

Now let us review all the prophetic Scriptures from Daniel, which were previously cited. Remember, Daniel had foretold of the time, *"they shall place the abomination that maketh desolate."*

After this, he compelled the Jews to worship as he directed. The certainty that Epiphanes desired to be worshipped as God seems obvious from his actions. The salutation of a letter written to Epiphanes and recorded by Josephus bears this out, "'To Antiochus **the god**, Epiphanes, a memorial from the Sidonians'."[104]

Many Jews compromised; many did not. Hundreds of thousands of those faithful Jews who refused to bow to this false god lost their lives. They were cruelly tortured. Just as God had foretold, *"They shall fall by the sword, and by flame, by captivity, and by spoil, many days."* The rest who compromised watched their brothers die.

Another of Daniel's prophesies foretold, *"But the people that do know their God shall be strong, and do exploits."* Five faithful Jewish brothers from the family of Maccabees led a

---

[a] Inner Holy Place.

[b] Jupiter was the Roman version of the Greek god, Zeus

revolt against this satanic tyrant. They taught God's law to the people just as Daniel had predicted; by God's strength they won.

In 165 B.C., three years after the statue of Jupiter was erected in the sanctuary, the Temple was cleansed under the leadership of Judas Maccabeas. Once again the Temple could be used for offerings. Judas is reputed to have said, "Let us go up to cleanse and dedicate the Sanctuary."[105]

Arnold G. Fruchtenbaum in his writings on Hanukkah points out a most remarkable prophetic fulfillment. He establishes the time from the murder of the rightful high priest, Onias III (171 B.C.)[a] until the time of the cleansing of the Temple by Judas Maccabeas. It was a span of exactly two thousand, three hundred days. This was just as Daniel had prophesied. *"Two thousand and three hundred days; then shall the sanctuary be cleansed."*[106]

Antiochus Theos Epiphanes died a slow, painful death from a disease of the bowels.

New Testament Celebration of Hanukkah

The New Testament mentions Hanukkah as one of the holy commemorative days being remembered by the Jews: *"And it was at Jerusalem the feast of the dedication, and it was winter. And Jesus walked in the Temple in Solomon's porch."*[b] (Note, the name Feast of Dedication is used, not the

---

[a] Remember, no sacrifices were valid if the high priest was not from the line ordained by God.

[b] John 10:22 Some expositors believe that because Jesus was in the Temple area during this time, he celebrated Hanukkah. However, this passage only states that Jesus was in the Temple area.

Festival of Lights. This suggests that in the first century, lights were still not a prominent part of Hanukkah which supports the previously mentioned legend premise.)

Actually, this short notation that Jesus was in the Temple area during Hanukkah offers important insight. This winter celebration occurred about four months before Passover and the coming Crucifixion. Why does the Bible mention where Jesus was and what message does Jesus bring at this specified time?

For three years, Jesus had walked among the people, teaching in the synagogues, healing the sick, and performing miracles. Almost no one really understood who Jesus was or that He had come to die. Through messengers, John the Baptist asked Jesus, *"Art thou he that should come, or do we look for another?"*[a] Peter came the closest to recognizing the deity of Christ when he acclaimed, *"Thou art the Christ, the Son of the living God."*[b]

It wasn't until after Jesus died and rose again that the disciples finally recognized Jesus as the Messiah, God in the flesh. However, they and many more Jews had followed Jesus with sincerity, desiring to understand who He was.

Other Jews followed Jesus but their motives were corrupt. Their purpose was to find some mistake, some weakness that would allow them to dismiss Jesus as the Promised One from God.

Who did Jesus speak to at Hanukkah? He addressed the unbelieving Jews. Notice, this encounter was the last time (recorded in John) that Jesus spoke to the masses. (After this, His messages were given only to the faithful.)

---

[a] Matthew 11:3

[b] Matthew 16:16

The question was asked by these Jews, "*How long dost thou make us to doubt? If thou be the Christ, tell us plainly.*"

The insincerity of this crowd is confirmed by the reply of Jesus. "*I told you, and ye believed not...ye believe not, because ye are not of my sheep...My sheep hear my voice, and I know them, and they follow me.*" Jesus then makes a statement that generates great hatred within these Jews: "*I and my Father are one.*"

Such anger arose within the men that they instantly tried to execute Jesus. "*Then the Jews took up stones again to stone him.*"[a] This was the second time the unbelieving Jews understood Jesus' claim to be God, and the second time they took up stones to kill Him.

Why did Jesus pick Hanukkah to tell this doubting crowd about His deity? Why was this the last time Jesus offered himself to the masses? Arthur Pink comments, "The mention of winter at this point is most significant and solemn. So far as they [the Jews] were concerned, the words of Jeremiah applied with direct and solemn force: *'The harvest is past, the summer is ended, and we are not saved'.*"[b][107]

God gives chilling insight into this type of crowd. "*Through deceit they refuse to know me, saith the Lord.*"[c]

Just as the first Hanukkah revealed massive unbelief and scant faith so we observe the same reactions at this last Hanukkah of Jesus. Three hundred years earlier, the unbelieving Jews had rejected God and joined together in worshipping Antiochus Epiphanes as God. During this

---

[a] John 10:24-31

[b] Jeremiah 8:20

[c] Jeremiah 9:6

first century celebration of Hanukkah, rejection of God occurred again.

Prophetic Impact of Hanukkah

Let us now compare biblically-prophesied future events to the persons and events that led up to Hanukkah. Especially recall the man Antiochus Epiphanes and the atrocities he committed. Most prophetic scholars consider Epiphanes to be a prepicture of the future Antichrist.

The book of Revelation describes a time period yet to come, in the plan of God. Throughout the Bible this seven-year period is described in scores of different terms. A few of the more familiar are the Tribulation, the Seventieth Week of Daniel, and the Time of Jacob's Trouble.[a]

As mentioned in the Yom Kippur chapter, the coming epoch of tribulation is a period when God once again turns His spotlight on His chosen people, the Jews. Just preceding this time, believers in Jesus Christ will be taken away in the Rapture. Soon after this exit of believers, a charming, but evil, political leader will draw the world together.

Among the impressive abilities he demonstrates is the supernatural expertise to uphold a seven-year covenant with the Jews. A close look at the passage informing us of this agreement gives us an interesting detail. *"And he shall confirm the covenant with many for one week."*[b] The correct

---

[a] Matthew 24:5-26; Daniel 9:24-27; Jeremiah 30:1-11

[b] Daniel 9:27 The Hebrew word "shabuwa," translated in this verse as "week," connotes a week of years (seven years). We see this definition verified in the length of time Jacob worked to earn Rachel as a wife. This time is described both as seven years and as one week. Genesis 29:20, 27, 28.

understanding of a Hebrew word in this verse gives great insight:

The Hebrew word "gabar," translated here in English "confirm," literally means "to strengthen" or "to prevail." Only once in the Bible is "gabar" translated confirm; it is in this verse. In the Bible, original treaties are said to be "made" or "established." We begin to see that the prophetic words, *he shall confirm the covenant*" do not say that a leader-to-come **makes** a covenant, but that a leader-to-come will **stand behind** (strengthen, prevail, validate or uphold) a covenant.

This seemingly small difference makes plausible the idea that the establishment of an agreement could occur even before the Rapture. Then, for some reason, the covenant does not become valid (or no one is able to enforce it) until this supernaturally endowed leader stands behind it for seven years.

We see that during this coming seven-year tribulation, this leader who arises will wear the mantle of previous man-god rulers. He will rule from an empire established out of countries which comprised the old Roman Empire. A comparison of land controlled by the Babylonian, Medo-Persian, Grecian, and Roman Empires shows they all encompassed much of the same territory. These are the empires prophetically outlined in Daniel.

Although this charmer, who in reality is the Antichrist, gains his position with promises of peace, he is unable to stall a worldwide disintegration for very long. Even with the aid of his miracle-working prime minister, "the false prophet,"[a] massive turmoil in the shape of war, famine, disease, and death will stalk the earth.[b]

It is intriguing to note in Daniel that this coming world leader will not regard "*the God of his fathers, nor the desire of women,[c] nor regard any god: for he shall magnify himself above all.*" This Scripture states that this satanically-led man will refuse to honor **any god** [which includes God the Father and Jesus]; instead he demands worship of himself. Wait! Look at the next verse. "*But in his estate [God's place], shall he honour the God of forces.*"[d] Who or what is this god that the Antichrist himself will worship?[e]

Many suggest that "God of Forces" describes the Antichrist as having a great army (because forces elsewhere is translated fortresses.) Maybe they are correct but verses 38 and 39 do not fit that interpretation very well.

The Antichrist will surely be a great military leader but the title God of Forces may be better recognized today as an idiom for "the god of nature" (as suggested by some

---

[a] Revelation 13

[b] Revelation, chapters 6-19, demonstrates the premise that although Satan desires to replace God, he is unable to fill the job description. Because Satan is a destroyer without the qualities of the only true God, ultimately he can only produce destruction in the lives of his subjects.

[c] Expositors such as J. Vernon McGee teach that "the desire of women" is a reference to Jesus because a) every Jewish woman wanted to be the mother of the Messiah and b) the phrase is located in the list of other gods he rejects. Others believe that this satanic character rejects relations with women because he is either a) a homosexual or b) a eunuch.

[d] Daniel 11:26-37

[e] Apparently Satan's offer (that Jesus refused) is accepted by the Antichrist. Satan offered world rulership in exchange for being worshiped as God. Matthew 4:7-10

commentators).[108] Scripture actually calls Satan *"the god of this world."*[a] Today, as we observe humankind moving deeper and deeper into earth worship, one has to ask, "Who actually is receiving this homage from mankind?" "Is worship of the god that Antichrist will honor materializing before our eyes?"

We know Satan is behind the scenes in this greatest of all spiritual battles. His counterfeit of the "holy trinity" consists of himself as God the Father, the Antichrist as God the Son (Savior), and the false prophet as the Holy Spirit. The god whom Antichrist worships in verses 38 and 39 must be Satan (cloaked perhaps in the garb of earth worship).

The spiritual dimension of this god-style dictatorship is not original. Its roots can be seen in the Garden of Eden. Remember Satan fell because of his desire to be God. Then, in turn, he offered a pseudo "godship" to Adam and Eve. If we follow the world empires from the tower of Babel down through the centuries, we see this idea of man being worshipped as God is a recurring theme. Throughout the Roman Empire, Caesar was worshipped as God. Most of all, in the life of Antiochus Epiphanes, we vividly see that desire to be worshipped.

The Bible tells us that the Antichrist will break his covenant with the Jews at the mid-point of the Tribulation. Jesus described this very event. He warned, *"When ye therefore shall see the abomination of desolation, spoken of by Daniel the prophet, stand in the holy place,"* you [the Jews] must abandon Jerusalem and run for your lives. He also warned, *"Then shall there be great tribulation, such as was not since the beginning of the world to this time, no, nor ever shall*

---

[a] II Corinthians 4:4

be."[a] This mid-point of the Tribulation holds great significance. At this time, the Antichrist:

1) Breaks his treaty with the Jews (Daniel 9:27)

2) Exalts himself above God (Daniel 11:36, 37)

3) Sits in the Temple, showing himself to be God (II Thessalonians 2:4)

4) Offers an abominable sacrifice in the Temple (Daniel 9:27; Matthew 24:15)

5) Requires the whole world to worship him (Revelation 13:7-18)

6) Begins a three and one half year attempt to kill the Jewish remnant who *"keep the commandments of God and have the testimony of Jesus Christ."* (Matthew 24:15-21; Revelation 12:4, 6, 13-17)

Now compare this coming Antichrist with his prophetic forerunner, Epiphanes. Epiphanes became king on a platform of peace, flattered and lied to gain advantage, used compromising Jews to gain his entrance to Jerusalem, desecrated the Temple, erected a statue of himself in the Temple, demanded to be worshipped as God, and killed multiplied thousands of Jews.

Hanukkah celebrates the time when God used Judas Maccabeas to destroy the evil Epiphanes, cleanse the Temple, and bring salvation to the Jews. Compare the cleansing of Hanukkah to the end of the Tribulation:

1) Jesus Christ returns to earth (Revelation 19:11-16)

---

[a] Matthew 24:15,21; Daniel 9:27

2) Jesus defeats the Antichrist (Revelation 19:20, 21)

3) Jesus rescues the believing Jews (Zechariah 14:3-9; Malachi 3:16-4:3)

At last, on earth we will see the destruction of the man-made world empires, and Jesus Christ will rule the earth from its capital city, Jerusalem. This marks the end of Gentile rule in Israel known as "the Times of the Gentiles."[a]

How perfectly the story of Hanukkah and the defeat of the vile Epiphanes show us prophetic events of the future.

Land For Peace

The Jewish people regained their land in 1948. To be accurate from the biblical perspective, let us say, "In 1948 they gained back a small sliver of their rightful land." Since this time of renewed statehood and renewed hope, the obstacles have been immense. As if it weren't enough to build a new country from nothing, the early builders themselves were just recovering from the worst instance of genocide in world history. From a motley gathering of survivors rose houses and farms and cities and a constitution and, most of all, a home; a home for the oppressed Jews of the world who for two thousand years had been displaced.

But the job was even more difficult because their Arab and Moslem neighbors refused to accept the presence of a

---

[a] The term "Times of The Gentiles" refers to the gap of time between the Gentile seizure of Israel in 607 B.C. and the Second Coming of Christ.

Jewish homeland in their midst. From the beginning, an economic boycott strangled the growth of Israel.

One has to wonder if God's directions had been followed more carefully in the past, would today's internal land struggles be as difficult? When the Jews first entered the Promised Land, God in His kindness warned about a potential problem: *"If ye will not drive out the inhabitants of the land from before you; then it shall come to pass, that those which ye let remain of them shall be pricks in your eyes, and thorns in your sides, and shall vex you in the land wherein ye dwell."*[a]

The Scriptures reveal that when the Jews first settled Israel, the inhabitants of Jerusalem were never totally driven out.[b] The battle inside Jerusalem continues today.

Another inside pocket of resistance that the Jews never finished rooting out was the land of the Philistines. Israel compromised on taking this territory. Incomplete obedience to God always comes back to haunt us. Today that spot of ground is called the **Gaza Strip**.

The attackers came. They came as snipers, as covert terrorist killers, and as members of large-scale, combined-military assaults. Yet through all these difficulties, the land and the people have survived. The land has exploded in population and expanded in borders. Repeated miracles demonstrating the providential hand of God have provided a fertile climate. This productive social and political climate has transformed the fledgling nation into a country that ranks in the top percentile in almost every area.

---

[a] Numbers 33:55

[b] Judges 1:21

Now, in the decade of the nineties, the whole world is focusing on the war-scarred land of Israel. Once again the question arises, who will reign in Jerusalem?[a]

Since the creation of man there have been wars. In every case, the unwritten law was, "To the victor belongs the spoil." For a reason that can ultimately only be found in the spirit realm, world opinion says that Israel should give back land gained in military victories. Why do nations ask Israel to return land when no other country returns theirs? This is a spiritual war. In a spiritual war, only spiritual answers will suffice.

Based on the lessons of Hanukkah, should the Jews hold their ground or compromise to get along? Human reason says, "If Israel doesn't compromise some, she can't survive," but what does God say about "land for peace?"

• God created the world and He designed Israel as His country. *"The land shall not be sold for ever: for the land is mine."*

• God chose Jerusalem as His capital city. *"Out of Zion shall go forth the law, and the word of the Lord from Jerusalem."*

• God ordained the Temple (and its location) as His Holy dwelling place. *"For now have I chosen and sanctified this house, that my name may be there for ever: and mine eyes and mine heart shall be there perpetually."*

The original instructions of God to the Jews were, "I will deliver the inhabitants of the land into your hand;

---

[a] One day after the historic 1993 handshake of Israeli Prime Minister Yitzhak Rabin and PLO Chairman Yasser Arafat on the White House lawn, the fight for Jerusalem surfaced. Arafat announced his plan as "the establishment of our independent Palestinian state with Jerusalem as its capital." AP Jerusalem

and thou shalt drive them out before thee. Thou shalt
make no covenant with them."[a]

Can Israel expect blessing from God if she trades away
God's property? Four thousand years ago, Abraham
wouldn't wait for God to provide the promised heir. He
used his own reasoning, had a child by another woman,
and produced Ishmael, the father of the Arabs. When
Abraham could no longer humanly propagate a child, God
stepped in and supernaturally gave Abraham the promised
child, Isaac. Today, will the children of Israel follow
Abraham's example of human reasoning to gain security
or will they wait for God's miracle? Where is Israel on
God's spiritual time clock?

If we are approaching the time of Jacob's Trouble, the
Tribulation, then the answers are clear. Israel will once
again make a league with the foreign nations around them
and will trust the lies of the coming Antichrist.[b] As we saw
in the prepictures of Epiphanes and Hanukkah, Israel will
be betrayed. But just as God sent Judas Maccabeas to
defeat Epiphanes, so God will send Jesus the Messiah to
once and for all free the Jews.[c] This future betrayal and
holocaust will be the last!

---

[a] Leviticus 25:23; Isaiah 2:2-4; II Chronicles 7:12, 16; Exodus 23:31-33

[b] It seems true that humankind does not learn much from history, let alone
from God. We keep making treaties with despotic murderers and then act surprised
when they betray our trust. England's famous diplomat, Neville Chamberlain,
negotiated a treaty with Hitler. Chamberlain said (while on his death bed during
a German air raid over England), **"Everything would have been allright if Hitler
hadn't lied to me."**

[c] Some in prophetic circles have conjectured that the cleansing of the Temple
(that must transpire after the Tribulation) might take place on Hanukkah. Perhaps
it will.

Personal Reactions To Prophecy

If reading about prophecy and the end of civilization as we know it today has put a scare into you, perhaps God is speaking to you. We have seen in this book that the atoning sacrifice of Jesus Christ is a truth presented throughout the whole Bible. Have you ever placed your faith in God's perfect Lamb, Jesus Christ? The familiar words of John 3:16 explain the plan God designed for you. *"For God so loved the world, that he gave his only begotton son, that whosoever believeth in him should not perish, but have everlasting life."*

Jesus is indeed the *"Lamb of God, which taketh away the sin of the world."*[a] In the Bible, God explains that access to Him is gained solely on the basis of our faith in Jesus, never on any human effort or works. *"For by grace are ye saved through faith; and that not of yourselves: it is the gift of God: not of works, lest any man should boast."*[b]

God said to look forward to the coming Rapture of believers. He promised this would be a **comforting** experience for us. If you ask God to allow Jesus to be **your** Savior, then the loving words of comfort offered to believers in Jesus Christ will be yours. Don't wait any longer to make this commitment. Time is running out for all of us.

---

[a] John 1:29

[b] Ephesians 2:8, 9

✡ ✡ ✡ ✡ ✡ ✡

SECTION V
PROHIBITIONS TO SPECIFIC DATING

The first four feasts of Israel describe in detail (including the timing) events connected with Christ's first coming. The remaining three feasts appear also to give details concerning His future Second Coming **even to exact days!** Information this specific, stands in direct contradiction to our traditional understanding of "date-setting."

Most Christians concur that it is useless to search for **exact dates** of end time occurrences. Reason dictates that it's foolish to try to determine the exact date of a biblical future event such as the Rapture, when the Bible itself states one cannot know the exact date.

A representative statement of the orthodox approach to "date setting" is found in *Bible Prophecy*, by Charles J. Woodbridge.

"THE TIME OF CHRIST'S COMING"
1. Due Caution

No man knows the exact hour of Jesus' return (Matthew 24:36,42). History tells us that occasionally people have forgotten or ignored our Savior's warning words. They have set dates for His return, put their affairs in order for an early departure from earth, and gathered at appointed centers to meet the Lord. Informed Christians however, know better than this. They always keep their affairs in order. They delight in anticipating Christ's return. But they are extremely careful not to set dates.

2. The Swift Immediacy of His Coming

Jesus will come *suddenly*, 'in a moment, in the twinkling of an eye' (I Corinthians 15:52). As the lightning flash (Matthew 24:27), or an unexpected thief (Matthew 24:43), or a snare (Luke 21:35), so will Christ's coming be. Think through each one of these comparisons. How rapid is the twinkling of an eye or a flash of lightning? How suddenly does a thief steal and then escape? How unexpectedly and quickly does a snare seize it's prey?"[109]

As you see, these words from Woodbridge reflect the position of most theologians. This viewpoint is pervasive and has had longevity. However, in light of the **specific prophetic fulfillments of numerous Jewish celebrations,** a review of the dating prohibition is in order.

CHAPTER 12
THIEF IN THE NIGHT

One familiar Bible verse used to dismiss the pursuit of specific prophetic dating is I Thessalonians 5:2, *"The day of the Lord so cometh as a thief in the night."* The prevailing interpretation of this Scripture has been, "Since one does not know when a thief is coming, one also cannot know when the Rapture will occur."

The first time I remotely considered reviewing any of these Scriptures was back in 1974. My spouse asked me the intriguing question; "Why do we Christians use I Thessalonians 5:2 to prove we can't date the Rapture, when verse 4, only two verses later says, *'But ye, brethren, are not in darkness, that that day should overtake you as a thief'?"* I couldn't answer.

I noted that another "thief" passage had a similar message. *"Remember therefore how thou hast received and heard, and hold fast, and repent. If therefore thou shalt not watch, I will come on thee as a thief, and thou shalt not know what hour I will come upon thee."*[a] It appeared that both of these "thief" Scriptures taught that Christians should not be surprised to see Jesus when He comes.

In 1975 we asked a noted prophetic author about the Thessalonians passage. "Why do preachers and Christian

---

[a] Revelation 3:3

movies use the theme *Thief in the Night* to teach a surprise Rapture, when I Thessalonians 5:4 says believers will not be surprised?"

He studied the section a moment and then replied, "I don't know." Although this author actually quotes I Thessalonians 5:4 in a book he wrote, he prefaces its use with, "We don't know when the Rapture will occur...but according to the signs, we are in the general time."

This encounter was significant because of this man's extensive studies of the end times. It was mystifying. Why have we all, including that dedicated prophetic teacher, applied the passage this way? This question led me to investigate further.

Interestingly, I found most scholars believe the passage in I Thessalonians 5 is not a direct reference to the Rapture. They reach this conclusion because of the specific term, "The Day of the Lord."[110] They feel the use of the phrase, The Day of the Lord, describes either (a) the whole seven-year period of judgment on the earth (along with the simultaneous seven-year preparation of the Bride in heaven); (b) the period from the Rapture to the end of the Millennium; or (c) the climactic end of the seven-year Tribulation.

A thoughtful study of all fifteen occurrences of "thief" in the New Testament produces an interesting profile. It seems **every** use of this word is in the negative. Even when the thief analogy does speak of Jesus, it typifies an unexpected appearance which brings about judgment to the unobservant slacker.

Examine three more examples of thief verses that relate to Jesus:

"And this know, that if the goodman of the house had known what hour the thief would come, he would have watched, and not have suffered his house to be broken through."

"The thief cometh not, but for to steal, and to kill, and to destroy: I am come that they might have life, and that they might have it more abundantly."

"Behold, I come as a thief. Blessed is he that watcheth, and keepeth his garments, lest he walk naked, and they see his shame."[a]

Notice, none of these thief verses suggest that Jesus comes as a surprise to those who are prepared and expectant. To the contrary, looking for Jesus Christ is referred to in Scripture as a "blessed hope"[b] not as a negative experience. There seems to be no scriptural justification to warrant the belief that Jesus will appear to obedient Christians as a thief. For your own verification, all New Testament thief verses are listed in the endnotes.[111]

One truth, however, can be clearly seen here. The Thessalonians "thief in the night" passage does teach that this appearance of Jesus will come as unexpectedly as a thief—to unbelievers.

Most importantly though, **this particular passage** does not teach that **Christians** cannot know the timing of future events! Based on this discovery, I decided to reexamine the other Scriptures that are supposed to prohibit exact dating of end-time events.[c]

---

[a] Luke 12:39; John 10:10; Revelation 16:15

[b] Titus 2:13

[c] This investigation took place over a fourteen year period. It took that long to come to the conclusions outlined in this book partly because of my reluctance to question long-held beliefs. It was difficult to "swim upstream," as it were, against the flow of conventional prophetic views. However for me, the freedom produced by these discoveries was worth the swim!

CHAPTER 13
WHAT WE CANNOT KNOW

The scriptural objection most often voiced to dating the Rapture is, "But the Bible says 'no man knows the day and the hour.'" Trying to compute these dates would certainly be futile:

(A) if these words from Jesus' speech to His disciples given on the Mount of Olives refer to the Rapture, and
(B) if they tell us **no one** could **ever** know exact dates of end-time events.

However, in studying the two occurrences of these words some surprising points emerged.

The first question that must be addressed is, "What 'hour' is being referred to in this statement?" In this chapter we will seek specifically to discover if these words from the Olivet discourse refer to the Rapture.

It is essential to notice that both occurrences of "No man knoweth the day or the hour" are **preceded** by these statements:

1. Matthew 24:29, "*Immediately <u>after the tribulation</u>...
Son of man coming in the clouds of heaven...*(verse 30)
all these things be fulfilled (verse 34)."

2. Mark 13:26 (after Jesus describes the awfulness of the Tribulation), "*then shall they see the Son of man coming in the clouds with great power and glory.*"

Notice also the companion passage in Luke 21:27, 31, (which records the same speech given in Matthew and Mark):

1. "*And then shall they see the Son of man coming in a cloud with power and great glory. So likewise ye, when ye see these things come to pass know ye that the Kingdom of God is nigh.*" (Note "after" and "and then" **follows** the description of the seven, long, painful years of tribulation.)

2. Notice the three previous Scriptures say, "*They shall see the Son of man coming in great power and glory.*" This information becomes vital since (by definition of the Rapture) Jesus is seen by everyone **only at His Second Coming.**

3. Jesus foretold in Luke 17:22-37 (after giving the analogies of the rescues of Noah and Lot), "*Even thus shall it be in the day when the Son of man is revealed.*" The revealing of the Son of man can only be the Second Coming, since Jesus is **not revealed** in the Rapture.

After looking at all three instances of this discourse in the Gospels, it appears that Jesus is teaching about His Second Coming and the end of the great Tribulation, not the Rapture.

Many Agree

It has been of particular interest to me to note the number of solid Bible teachers who have expressed this same viewpoint regarding these passages. Following are the statements of just four of them:

1. Harry A. Ironside states in his book *Matthew*, with regard to chapter 24, "The secret of the Rapture of the Church, prior to the end-time, is not introduced here in this great prophetic discourse. That was still a hidden mystery when Jesus spoke these words." Referring to finding the Rapture in Matthew, chapter 24, he continues "There is no time set for it, nor are there any signs indicated. The signs here all have to do with His revelation from heaven as the King who is to return to take His great power and reign. The coming of the Son of man refers always to this event, **never to the Rapture!**"[a][112]

2. Arno C. Gaebelein writes concerning Matthew 24 in his book, *The Gospel of Matthew,* "We say once more that this has nothing to do with the Church. The removal of the Church takes place before the last day of Daniel's prophecy begins and when the Lord comes immediately after the days of tribulation, the Church is with Him and in His Glory the Church is manifested. The revelation concerning His coming for the Church is recorded in I Thessalonians 4:15-18. To make the elect in Matthew 24:30 the Church, as it is done so often, is

---

[a] Emphasis mine.

bewildering and a wrong interpretation.[a] This part of the Olivet discourse, as we have shown, has nothing whatever to do with the Church."[113]

3. John Walvoord teaches in *Matthew—Thy Kingdom Come*, "Those who believe that the Rapture, or translation of the Church, occurs before the time of trouble at the end of the age, usually do not believe the Rapture is in view at all in this discourse, as the Rapture was first introduced in John 14:1-3, sometime after the Olivet discourse...If the details of this discourse are observed and interpreted literally, it fits best with the view that the Rapture is not revealed in this discourse at all, but is a later revelation, introduced by Christ in John 14 and revealed in more detail in I Corinthians 15 and I Thessalonians 4.

"The entire passage from Matthew 24:15-31 is the specific answer to the disciples of the sign of His coming and of the end of the age, with the climactic sign being the Second Coming and the glory that attends it, and will fulfill the prophecy of Acts 1:11 that Christ will return as He went up into heaven, that is, His return will be physical, gradual, visible, and with clouds. Matthew 24:31 brings to a close the first doctrinal section of the Olivet discourse, and what follows is a series of applications and illustrations.

"In interpreting the illustrations which follow, while there may be secondary applications of the truth to the Church awaiting the Rapture,

---

[a] Emphasis mine.

the laws of exegesis[a] would dictate that the
illustrations should relate to the doctrine of the
Second Coming of Christ."[114][b]

4. Referring to Matthew 24:40, 41 J. Vernon McGee
remarks in *Matthew*, "I can hear someone saying to
me, 'Well preacher, you have finally painted
yourself into a corner. You said **the Church and
the Rapture are not in the Olivet discourse**[c] and
here they are. Two shall be in the field and one
shall be taken and the other shall be left.'" McGee
repeats, "**This is not a reference to the Rapture of
the Church.**"[115][d]

Again and again I've heard noted radio Bible teachers
say, "We used to believe these Scriptures in the Olivet
discourse were referring to the Rapture, but we see now
that this is a section on the Second Coming of Jesus."
This knowledge alone should caution us not to use
Matthew 24:36 or Mark 13:32 as proof texts that no one can
"know the day or the hour" of the **Rapture.**

Does Noah "Sink" This Premise?

Some hold to the thought that the "coming" spoken of
in Matthew 24 must be the Rapture because of the

---

[a] A critical explanation of a portion of Scriptures.

[b] Emphasis mine.

[c] Emphasis mine.

[d] Emphasis mine.

reference to Noah's time. Verses 37-39 say, "*But as the days of Noe[a] were, so shall also the coming of the Son of man be. For as in the days that were before the flood they were eating and drinking, marrying and giving in marriage, until the day that Noe entered into the ark, and knew not until the flood came, and took them all away; so shall the coming of the Son of man be.*"

They say, "The comparison made here by Jesus is that Noah's time was the same as the time before the Rapture. People in Noah's day are described as eating, drinking and marrying, living life as usual." They explain, "It has to be the Rapture since the Second Coming described in Revelation is at the end of the Tribulation and since that time will be so terrible, as God rains down successive judgments from heaven, in no way could you describe it as 'life as usual.'"

In answer to this thought, I'd like to suggest that "life as usual" can have several meanings. First of all, let's take a close look at the people who were destroyed in both the flood and Sodom and Gomorrah.

In Noah's day we see rampant sin and disregard for any of God's restraints. God's description of the antediluvian[b] population just before the flood paints a desperately evil time. Granted, it was not a time exactly like the end of the Tribulation will be, but it had to be somewhat similar. People running amuck without any godly restraint had created a world problem so bad that the Bible states that "*it repented the Lord that He had made man on the earth.*" In fact God describes seeing "*that the wickedness of man was great in the earth, and that every*

---

[a] New Testament spelling of Noah.

[b] Those living before the flood.

imagination of the thoughts of his heart was only evil continually."[a]

That life goes on without any thought for the God who created them, is what I believe this New Testament Scripture is emphasizing.

The "life being lived as if God didn't exist" interpretation of this passage as well as "life as usual" holds true in Lot's example, also. Life just before the destruction of Sodom and Gomorrah could hardly be described as normal. Men in Sodom were so taken in the depravity of homosexuality that even being struck blind by God did not deter them from trying to pollute the bodies of the "new men in town."[b] Indeed, the "life as usual" pictured in the time before the flood and the population destroyed in Lot's day certainly are not "pastoral pictures."

The Bible describes the last days as "perilous times,"[c] yet, in a sense, life does go on even during the Tribulation. God says there will be buying and selling.[d] In fact, just before Jesus' Second Coming described in Revelation 19, we see mention of kings, merchants, rich men, shipmasters, and sailors, as well as great cities, wealth, slavery, musicians, craftsmen, bridegrooms, brides, and nations.[e] All these indicate that even though the

---

[a] Genesis 6:5, 6

[b] Genesis 19:1-11

[c] II Timothy 3:1-7

[d] Revelation 13:16, 17

[e] Revelation 18:9-24

judgments from God devastate both mankind and our planet, man continues to carry on his earthly activities.[a]

Timing of Noah and the Flood

Another piece of information that bolsters the Second Coming view of Matthew 24 is the sequence of events in Genesis when Noah entered the ark. A close study of Genesis chapter 7 (particularly verses 2-4, 7, 8, 10, and 16) shows us that 1) Noah and his family boarded the ark, 2) the animals went in, 3) God shut the door, 4) everyone inside waited seven days, 5) the rain began, and 6) all air-breathing antediluvian life not on the ark drowned.

The verses supporting this viewpoint of flood events are thirteen and fourteen which clarify that people and animals all entered the ark on the same day; verse seven which says Noah and company went in; and verse ten which informs us, *"and it came to pass after seven days, that the waters of the flood were upon the earth."* If this suggested scenario is correct, then Matthew 24:37-39 shows us in (type) the destruction of antediluvian society being compared to the destruction of the Tribulation population.

Some still may feel the Rapture must be contained inside the Olivet discourse because the population in Noah's day is described as enjoying life. Those who perceive the horrible time at the end of the Tribulation to be just too terrible to be described as "life as usual" must consider the impact of the timing of Noah's rescue.

We cannot discount the important interval of time between Noah's rescue and the actual destruction of the flood. *"Until the day that Noah entered into the ark, and knew*

---

[a] Compare the Egyptian society (government and military) continuing even after a succession of devastating disasters. Exodus 7-14.

not until [seven days later] *the flood came and took them all away.*"[a]   Again, even though the pre-flood populace was described in Noah's day to be thoroughly rotten, they still had the seven days to encounter changes while Noah rested safely in the ark. These seven days could easily typify the hard times of the Tribulation.

The Reason for Reference to Noah's Day

It seems more likely that Jesus' comparison of Noah's and Lot's generations to the future unbelieving generation concerns their **"know-not" status.**

We know by reading II Peter 2:5 that the population in Noah's day heard about the impending judgment, but did not believe the warning. *"And spared not the old world, but saved Noah the eighth person, a <u>preacher</u> of righteousness, bringing in the flood upon the world of the ungodly."* This attitude of unbelief is repeated in the behavior of the people living during the Tribulation as they will choose to blaspheme God rather than repent and be saved. They actually do not believe God will ultimately judge them. In rebellion, they go out to war against Him.

Revelation says, they *"repented not of their deeds,"* and *"I saw the beast, and the kings of the earth, and their armies, gathered together to make war against him that sat on the horse, and against his army."*[b]

We also see this determined attitude of unbelief in II Peter 3:3-7, *"Knowing this first, that there shall come in the last days scoffers walking after their own lust;*

---

[a]   Matthew 24:38, 39

[b]   Revelation 16:11, 19:19

And saying, Where is the promise of his coming? for since the fathers fell asleep, all things continue as they were from the beginning of the creation.

For this they <u>willingly are ignorant</u> of, that by the word of God the heavens were of old, and the earth standing out of the water and in the water:

Whereby the world that then was, being overflowed with water, perished:

But the heavens and the earth, which are now, by the same word are kept in store, reserved unto fire against the day of judgment and perdition of ungodly men."

I believe the Matthew 24 passage teaches that **life was as usual** *"until the day that Noe entered the ark."* Then, referring to the population shut outside of the ark, they *"knew not until the flood came and took them all away."* They "knew not" what? They "knew not" that they were going to be destroyed by God! The same attitude of disbelief concerning impending destruction will exist before the Second Coming of Christ. The scoffing generation of II Peter 3:3-7 that will receive the seven years of Revelation judgment from God, is said to be *"willingly ignorant"* of the impending judgment.

The rest of chapter 24 and the whole of chapter 25 continues to contrast those who know and expect Jesus' return with those who don't care and postpone getting right with God, thus receiving judgment.

The story of Noah is such a beautiful picture of the preservation of believers. Throughout Noah's life, God gave successively more detailed information about the impending judgment and God's promised rescue of Noah and his family. This information is listed in Genesis 5-8.

Information first came through the name Enoch gave to his son. This name "Methuselah" means, "When he is gone it will come." The flood actually came the year that

Methuselah died! Then God gave the promise of 120 years yet to come. Next, God sent the animals to Noah, told him to load the food supply, and last He gave the invitation to step aboard. Noah was also given the **exact time** of the judgment of the earth in Genesis 7:7, *"For yet seven days and I will cause it to rain upon the earth."*[a]

This principle, of God **telling believers** shortly before He rescues them from the judgment of unbelievers, is suggested in Amos 3:7. *"Surely the Lord God will do nothing, but he revealeth his secret unto his servants the prophets."*[b]

We see this again, demonstrated in God's foretelling Abraham about His plan to destroy Sodom and Gomorrah.[c] After informing Abraham, God sent angels **to warn Lot** about the impending destruction. These angels advised Lot, *"Whatsoever thou hast in the city, bring them out of this place: For we will destroy this place."* Lot quickly informed his family about imminent doom. His sons-in-law discounted the whole story as a big joke choosing not to believe a word Lot said.

The next morning the angels hurried Lot and his three family members who did believe the warning out of the city. *"Then the Lord rained upon Sodom and upon Gomorrah*

---

[a] A possible allusion to the Rapture in this whole flood scenario is that Noah represents the raptured believers. This is seen in the fact that seven days before the total judgment upon mankind, the Lord called Noah into the ark and the Lord shut the door. Genesis 7:1,4,16.

[b] Although some teachers maintain that this Scripture only applies to the prophets of God who recorded God's messages in the Bible, the ultimate conclusion remains the same. God through His word (via human scribes) gives believers information concerning the future (including impending judgments).

[c] Genesis 18:17-33

brimstone and fire from the Lord out of heaven." The sons-in-law died.[a]

Again, we see progressive understanding[b] given to believers concerning their rescue from the impending judgment coming against unbelievers.

The comparison of the unaware, uncaring, unbelieving population who lived in the city of Sodom just before it was destroyed by God to the population that is judged by God at the end of the Tribulation is made by Jesus in Luke 17:28-30. *"Likewise also as it was in the days of Lot; they did eat, they drank, they bought, they sold, they planted, they builded;*

But the same day that Lot went out of Sodom it rained fire and brimstone from heaven and destroyed them all.

Even thus shall it be in the day when the Son of man is revealed."[c]

This principle of **telling believers ahead of time** about being rescued from impending destruction is summed up by Jesus.[d] After telling the disciples what would transpire during the seven-year Tribulation, He summed up how believers should respond to this awesome information. *"And when these things begin to come to pass, then look up, and lift up your heads; for your redemption draweth nigh."*

---

[a] Genesis 19:14-16

[b] Since the completion of the Scriptures in A.D. 90 , "new" information comes from a clearer and deeper understanding of the Bible.

[c] Note this depiction, "the Son of man revealed," is a description of the bodily, visible Second Coming of Jesus, not the call of Jesus for believers called the Rapture.

[d] Luke 21:28

One Taken—One Left

Some Bible expositors see the Rapture in Matthew 24 for a different reason. They hold the thought that the latter part of the Olivet discourse of Jesus in Matthew 24:40-51 (repeated in Luke 17:30-37) is a definite picture of the Rapture of the believers. Calling this "the Rapture section" is based on the "*one taken—one left*" illustrations of Matthew 24:40 and 41.

This conclusion is based on the Greek word "airo" which is "to lift, to take up or away" translated into English "took" in Matthew 24:39. "*And knew not until the flood took them all away.*" This "took" is about the populace who died in the flood and is an obvious reference to judgment.

Next it is pointed out that the word "taken" as used in the following verses is the Greek word "paralambano" which means "to receive near, to associate with oneself." They insist that the word "paralambano" is **always and only** used in a positive or friendly sense.

"*Then shall two be in the field; the one shall be taken, and the other left.*

Two women shall be grinding at the mill; the one shall be taken, and the other left."

They say these people are taken up with Jesus. They do not see the "taken ones" as going into Judgment (which would make it a Second Coming passage).

Since "paralambano" is formed by combining "para" (meaning "near" or "beside") with "lambano" (meaning "to take"), they conclude that the compound word produced could not be used to describe people being taken away in judgment.

It is then expertly pointed out that this **same word, "paralambano"** is translated into English in John 14:3 as "receive." The importance of this, they say, is that "the word paralambano is selected by Jesus to describe taking the Church to himself, just as He used it earlier in Matthew 24."

Judgment or Heaven

At first sight this viewpoint is convincing. However, a study of **every** use of the Greek word "paralambano" in the Bible reveals an interesting insight. Paralambano is used forty-eight times in the New Testament. Interestingly, fourteen uses of it describe the taker or the destination as **negative.** Examples of this use are, *"Then the devil taketh him," "Then goeth he, and taketh with himself seven other spirits more wicked than himself" and "They took Jesus and led him away."*[a]

John F. Walvoord comments about the premise that "paralambano" is always used in a friendly sense in *The Rapture Question.* He states this premise "is destroyed by the fact that the same word is used in John 19:16-17 in reference to taking Jesus to the cross, an obvious act of judgment which contradicts the statement that the word is always used in a friendly sense."[116]

The conclusion that the people in Matthew 24:40, 41 are taken into judgment seems to fit the context of the passage best. The last two verses of this chapter describe the **punishment** of those who are not ready when the lord of the servant returns. *"The lord of that servant shall come in a day when he looketh not for him, and in an hour that he is not aware of, and shall cut him asunder, and appoint him his portion*

/

---

[a] Matthew 4:5, 12:45; John 19:26

with the hypocrites; there shall be weeping and gnashing of teeth."[a]

The passage in Luke is even more direct in explaining that the people who are "taken" in the Olivet discourse are taken to judgment. *"I tell you, in that night there shall be two men in one bed; the one shall be taken, and the other shall be left.*

Two women shall be grinding together; the one shall be taken, and the other shall be left.

Two men shall be in the field; the one shall be taken, and the other shall be left.

And they answered and said unto him, Where Lord? And he said unto them, whithersoever the body is, thither will the eagles be gathered together."[b] Based on the symbolism throughout the Bible of eagles gathering to devour dead bodies, this surely sounds like judgment![c]

Compare Jesus' answer in Luke to the Second Coming judgment. *"And he cried with a loud voice, saying to all the fowls that fly in the midst of heaven, Come and gather yourselves unto the supper of the great God; That ye may eat the flesh of kings...of captains...of mighty men...of horses...of them that sit on them...of all men free and bond, both great and small."*[d]

One more difficulty of calling the "one taken—one left" section of Luke 17:20-36 a "Rapture section" is found in verse thirty. It precedes the "one taken—one left" passage and states: *"Thus shall it be in the last day when the Son of man is revealed."* This has to be the time at the end of the seven-

---

[a] Matthew 24: 50, 51

[b] Luke 17:34-37

[c] Job 39:27-30; Matthew 24:28

[d] Revelation 19:17, 18

year Tribulation when *"every eye shall see"* Jesus coming back in His glorious Second Coming.

The "one taken" of the Olivet discourse must of necessity be those living on earth who have taken the mark of the beast, as well as those who have refused to believe that Jesus was ever coming back. These will be taken away into judgment. They will not be left with the believing remnant who will populate the earth during Jesus' millennial reign of peace.[a]

Indeed, it appears most likely that Jesus' words, "No man knoweth the day or the hour" is a reference to His Second Coming, **not to the Rapture.**[b]

---

[a] Revelation 1:7, 19:17-21

[b] How amazing to observe the countless teachers and preachers who definitely believe that the Rapture is not contained in the Olivet discourse, yet, they still continue to pull out the one verse "No man knows the day nor the hour" as a prooftext for not being able to know the date of the Rapture!

CHAPTER 14
CAN'T KNOW NOW OR EVER

Some will quickly note, "Well if this 'day and hour' that we can't know is the Second Coming, it doesn't work scripturally! If we could know the exact Rapture date, we could determine the exact day of the Second Coming right now. We could simply add the seven years of Tribulation to discover the date that Jesus said no one could know!

Yes, that would be true, except for two reasons.

First, do we have an abundance of Scriptures that prove that the countdown for the seven years of Tribulation begins at the exact moment of the Rapture?

Second, even if we couldn't know the day of the Rapture, anyone living during the seven-year Tribulation could count 1,260 days from the "abomination" spoken of in Daniel, chapter 9 and Revelation, chapter 12 to discover the **exact day** of the Second Coming. These people would then know what the Bible says they can't know!

That puts a real twist in our interpretation of what we can and cannot know.

A Reasonable Answer

As we ponder this question let us also review the second part of the original question in chapter 11. Does Jesus tell us in the Olivet discourse that **no one but God**

would ever know the exact day and hour of the Rapture and of the Second Coming? This is a **vital factor** to consider before we can comfortably use these passages to rule out ever knowing a specific Rapture date.

The twenty-fourth chapter of Matthew begins with the disciples questioning Jesus: *"Tell us, when shall these things be? and what shall be the sign of thy coming, and of the end of the world?"*

Jesus doesn't answer their questions immediately, but instead He describes many awesome events that would occur before His coming and the end of the world. His discourse begins in verse four and continues through verse thirty-five. Only then does Jesus finally answer the disciples' original question. He states; *"But of that day and hour knoweth no man, no, not the angels in heaven."* Notice the exact information given to His disciples. It is: Neither angels nor men knew the day of His coming.

Consider Jesus

While we consider the accuracy of this observation, look at the parallel passage in Mark 13:32, *"But of that day and that hour knoweth no man, no, not the angels which are in heaven, neither the Son, but the father."* Note here that not only angels and men are listed as not knowing the date of the Second Coming of Jesus, but the **Son** also names himself as not knowing! This piece of information makes the whole search very intriguing.

If we decide that these two passages teach that no person could **ever** know the day and hour of the Second Coming, then we would also have to conclude that Jesus would not know the date of His departure for the Rapture until its exact moment!

We need to take a moment to consider how the Son of God, Jesus, very God himself, could **ever** not know anything.

Many Bible scholars feel that from the time Jesus was born of a virgin, walked the earth, was tempted, died, was resurrected, and once again ascended to the Father, He chose to set aside and not use His powers of the Godhead. They believe Jesus willingly elected not to exercise His powers of omnipresence, omnipotence, and omniscience, even though He still was God.

J. Vernon McGee comments on this verse in *Mark*. "This verse is admittedly difficult. If Jesus is God, it is difficult to account for this lack of omniscience. *'Neither the Son'* is added by Mark (compare Matthew 24:36). Mark presents Jesus as *'the servant, and the servant knoweth not what his Lord doeth.'* The servant character of Jesus represents His most typical and true humanity. He *'took on the form of a servant.'* When He became a man, He limited Himself in order to be made like us. He **was not omnipresent when He became man.**"[117]

There are other examples of Scriptures that lead to this belief. Luke 2:52 states, *"Jesus increased in wisdom."* This infers that Jesus had to study just as we do. Of course the meaning of Hebrews 4:15, *"but was in all points tempted like as we are,"* becomes a greater reality to us knowing that Jesus must have been tempted not to persevere in scriptural studies much as we are tempted.

This "setting aside" of godly attributes is further deduced from Jesus' potential to be tempted, His need to be ministered to, His increase in strength of spirit, His need for food, His calling upon God for miracles, His thirst, and His being fashioned as a man.[a]

Scripture makes clear the depth of commitment the very God, Jesus, made to come live, die, and rise again in order to provide salvation for us. *"For verily he took not on him the nature of angels; but he took on him the nature of Abraham. Wherefore in all things it behoved him to be made like unto his brethren, that he might be a merciful and faithful high priest in things pertaining to God, to make reconciliation for the sins of the people."*[b]

One of the passages previously mentioned that indicates this voluntary setting aside of godly capabilities actually concerns prophetic dates.[c] Jesus explained, *"...knoweth no man...neither the son."* This statement of Jesus conclusively proves that He did not know everything **(at least when He spoke these words)**. This verse also seems to infer that He was not using His omniscience as He spoke to His disciples. Since the Bible is very clear that Jesus is God, then the only way He could not have *"known the day or the hour"* as He spoke was, as Philippians 2:5-8 states, because of His voluntary temporary submission to live in the humble form of a human.

Most importantly, note Jesus's answer in Mark to the disciples' question of, *"When shall these things be?"* He answers, *"Of that day and hour knoweth no man, no, not the angels which are in heaven, neither the Son, but the Father."* He does **not** say, "I will **never** know the day nor hour, neither will any man."

---

[a] Matthew 4:1, 2, 11; Luke 2:40, 52, 24:41-43; John 11:41, 42, 19:28; Philippians 2:5-8

[b] Hebrews 2:16-18

[c] Mark 13:32

Concluding that Jesus would never know the day or hour until the moment of departure in order to hold on to the "it's impossible to date" idea, produces an insurmountable problem. Even if Jesus were not to be told His departure day until the day arrived, He could quite easily compute it ahead of time. He could count days either from the inception of the Tribulation or from the moment He saw the Abomination of Desolation occur.[a] He would need only to apply His knowledge of the Scriptures in Daniel and Revelation to calculate the number of days.

God prophetically outlined more than one benchmark event in the Seventieth Week of Daniel. One mark given is at the beginning of the seven-year period. This is when the Antichrist confirms a covenant with the nation of Israel. Another definite mark occurs at the mid-point of the seven years when the Antichrist stands in the Temple demanding to be worshipped as God.

Actually **biblical date setting** could be done by others besides Jesus! Using the information from Daniel, dates could be calculated by the 144,000 Jews who are sealed during the seven-year Tribulation.[b] In fact, during the Tribulation, anyone who looked into the prophetic Scriptures could calculate the **exact day** of Jesus' Second Coming!

Some defenders of the "can't-ever-know" belief seek to dilute this powerful information by saying, "Well, because the Tribulation will be so terrible, God cuts the seven years short. Since no one knows how much He will cut off, no

---

[a] As outlined in Hanukkah chapter, the Abomination of Desolation describes the point in time that the Antichrist will stand in the Temple, demanding to be worshipped as God. Daniel 9:27; II Thessalonians 2:4.

[b] Revelation 7; 14:1-5

one could calculate from an indefinite time period." They
use as biblical support Jesus' prophetic words in the Olivet
discourse, "*Except those days should be shortened, there should
no flesh be saved: but for the elect's sake those days shall be
shortened.*"[a]

Jesus' statement that "*those days shall be shortened*" is
intriguing indeed. He is definitely teaching about the
Tribulation in this passage, but what exactly does He
mean? Some suggest He means that the actual days
themselves will be less than 24 hours long. Others endorse
the "shortening of the seven-year period" concept. I think
a better explanation of His words might be found by
referring back to the information Jesus just gave in the
preceding verse.[b] He warned, "*For then shall be great
tribulation, such as was not since the beginning of the world to
this time, no, nor ever shall be.*"[c]

Examine this passage in your Bible. You will see that
verses 21 and 22 are joined together by the word "and." In
essence, He is saying, "This horrible part of the Tribulation
(after the mid-point) will be so bad that if it were not
shortened no one would survive." I believe the shortening
that occurs might be a direct reference to the length of
time **during the Tribulation** in which God pours out His
wrath on the unbelieving world.

To select the premise that the Seventieth Week of
Daniel would ever be less that seven years long does great

---

[a] Matthew 24:22

[b] One of the easiest and most accurate tools of Bible study is to read a verse in
"context." Read the Scriptures before and after the verse in question and usually
the meaning of the verse in question becomes clear.

[c] Matthew 24:21 Note that verse 15 puts the "then shall be great tribulation"
event after the mid-point of the Tribulation so the time shortened must be in the
latter half of the seven years.

injustice to the miraculous design of the Holy Scriptures. Even the time period of seven years originates from prophecy in Daniel. In the Daniel passage, one can clearly see (after a bit of serious study, I must admit) that God promised to work with His people, the Jews, for a total of four hundred and ninety years. He also prophesied that after the first four hundred and eighty-three years, Messiah would come, but He would be killed. The time clock for the four hundred and ninety years would then stop for an undetermined interval after which God would continue the countdown and complete the remaining seven years. God gave His word, which cannot and will not be broken, so we should expect the Tribulation to be seven years long—to the day.

Let us review the specific information given in the Bible about the duration of the seventieth week of Daniel. To assure our understanding of this time, God used assorted methods of measurement to describe the exactness of its length:

1) The first half is 1260 days long.[a]
2) The second half is 1260 days long.[b]
3) The second half is forty-two months long.[c]

---

[a] Revelation 11:3

[b] Revelation 12:6 Note God's original year, as well as the original Jewish year, contained 360 days. Seven years would then contain exactly 2520 days. The 2520 day total (for seven years) is the same as the first half of 1260 days added to the second half of 1260 days.

[c] Revelation 11:2 Eighty-four months equal seven years, so forty-two months equal exactly half of seven years.

4) The length of the second half is said to be, "*a time, and times, and half a time.*"[a]
5) It is one week long.[b]

God made sure mankind understood the exact length of this yet-to-be-fulfilled prophetic time period. He believes the length to be important; so should we.

Some teachers are so set against believing that God would reveal future dates to His children that they put forth what appear to be unbiblical statements to strengthen their position. These kinds of statements spill out. "I believe that if we ever did figure out the timing of future events God would change His schedule just to show us that He is still in control."

How odd to state such a belief when Scriptures tell us that many thousands of years ago, God set exact moments in time when He would carry out His plans. For example God states, "*The four angels were loosed, which were prepared for an hour, and a day, and a month, and a year, for to slay the third part of men.*"[c] Here we see God's precise, prescribed, prophetic plans for the future. An additional passage reveals the longevity of God's plans. "*For ever, O Lord, thy word is settled in heaven.*"[d]

---

[a] Daniel 7:25, 12:7; Revelation 12:14 A "time" in these passages equals one year. That means, one time + two times + one half a time equals three and one half years (or half of seven years).

[b] Daniel 9:27 In Hebrew the word "week" in this passage literally means "sevens of years".

[c] Revelation 9:15

[d] Psalm 119:89

Times and Seasons

Serious students of prophecy, who hold the belief, "You can know the general time and the seasons of the Rapture but definitely not the day and the hour," must consider yet another Scripture.

Just before Jesus was taken up into heaven, His disciples asked, *"Wilt thou at this time restore again the kingdom to Israel?"* Oh no! Here the disciples go again, asking Jesus to give them the time of Israel's kingdom age. Please note carefully every word of Jesus' reply to them *"And He said unto them, 'It is not for you to know the <u>times or the seasons,</u> which the Father hath put in his own power."* It's interesting to note that according to *Strong's Exhaustive Concordance* the word "time" in this verse come from the Greek root word "kairos" which means "set or proper time" while the word translated "seasons" comes from the Greek word "chronos" which means "a space of time." The translators saw a difference in the meaning of the two words as they are used in this verse. "Time" refers to an **occasion** and "seasons" is a specific (but larger) **expanse of time.** In the same way the word "chronos" is used in Acts 14:17 and translated fruitful "seasons."

Do you see the problem that this verse presents? We are informed from Scriptures[a] about the kind of conditions that will exist in the last days. This means that the **general time of the end can be known** by believers, yet Acts 1:7 says the **times and the seasons cannot be known!** Could it be, as previously discussed, that the prohibition to know

---

[a] II Timothy 3:1-5

the exact hour of end-time occurrences applied only to believers of Jesus' day?

Considering all of the preceding information, it appears the solid information that we derive from "*no man knoweth the day or the hour*" is that A) Jesus is referring to the Second Coming **not the Rapture** and B) **only at the time Jesus spoke these words** was the date known exclusively by God the Father.

CHAPTER 15
HIDDEN INFORMATION

The logical thought occurring in most Christians' minds at this point is, "If the application of these Scripture passages in regard to specific Rapture dating is correct, then why haven't any theologians throughout the centuries discovered this interpretation?"

This question is indeed appropriate when one considers the universality of the historic misapplication of the Rapture to both I Thessalonians, chapter 5 and Matthew, chapter 24.

Could the reason for this strange, two thousand year old misunderstanding be a demonstration of the perfect timing of God? Might He have closed our discernment of some verses and allowed a misunderstanding to exist among Christians for almost two thousand years?

A key section on prophecy demonstrates this principle of withholding understanding. The Scriptures read, "*But thou, O Daniel, shut up the words, and seal the book, even to the time of the end...And I heard, but I understood not: then said I, O my Lord, what shall be the end of these things? And he said, Go thy way, Daniel: for the words are closed up and sealed till the time of the end.*"[a]

---

[a] Daniel 12:4, 8, 9

If God had allowed us to decipher the exact dates long before the actual time of the end, then the admonition to the Church to "be ready" would have been ineffective as a spur to remain faithful.

It is interesting to note the observations of J. A. MacDonald on this subject in *The Pulpit Commentary*. After a discussion on whether or not God reveals the future to believers, he writes, "Wisdom withholds particular revelations of the future to encourage prayer. Yet it is generally made known to the wise." He concludes, "The wise who study this series [of events prophesied to precede Jesus' coming] cannot be ignorant as to the approaching time. But to the wicked it will come as a surprise."[118]

Note that even though Jesus told His disciples that the Holy Spirit would *"guide you into all truth"* and that *"he will show you things to come,"*[a] the men who heard these words did not necessarily comprehend everything they heard or even wrote. John, who recorded this promise of the coming Spirit, also observed the Revelation of Jesus Christ. Jesus in this revelation instructed John simply to record what he saw. There is no indication that John, nor the prophetic writers of the Old Testament, actually understood all the fulfillments or timing of the visions given to them by God.

It is consistent with God's other dealings with mankind to seal up the information in Daniel (and other end time prophesies) until He is ready to reveal it to His children. Note how Paul prefaced his words revealing the Rapture, *"Behold, I show you a mystery."* This indicates the unveiling of a truth not previously revealed to or understood by mankind. Through Paul, God then proclaims a beautiful promise to believers of the newly initiated Church Age.

---

[a] John 16:13

"We shall not all sleep, but we shall all be changed, In a moment, in the twinkling of an eye, at the last trump: for the trumpet shall sound, and the dead shall be raised incorruptible, and we shall be changed."[a]

Some theologians flatly state, "The church is not seen in the Old Testament." These expositors believe that no event relating to the Church can be found in the Old Testament because the Church is "a mystery yet unrevealed."

In considering this vital issue, we must first note, according to *The New Bible Dictionary*, "In the New Testament *mysterion*[b] signifies a secret which is being, or even has been, revealed, which is also divine in scope, and needs to be made known by God to men through His Spirit."[119]

The prevailing theological interpretation is that a "mystery" in Scripture is a previously hidden truth, now divinely revealed.[c]

Some interpret this definition of "previously hidden truth" to mean that "mysteries" **are not even referred to in the Scriptures** before the time of their unveiling. This belief leads to pronouncements such as, "The Church is not found in the Feasts of Israel." This conclusion, based on the use of "mystery" seems inaccurate, especially since some of the twenty-five New Testament appearances of "mystery/mysteries" describe subjects which first appeared in the Old Testament. For example, notice the I Timothy 3:16 "mystery" reference of the pre-existence, incarnation and work of Jesus, yet almost the whole book of Hebrews

---

[a] I Corinthians 15:51, 52

[b] The Greek word from which we get the English word, mystery

[c] For an example see Scofield Referrence Bible notes, Matt. 13 # 3.

unveils the **pre-figurements of Jesus in The Tabernacle and Old Testament types.**

Could God be calling these subjects "mysteries" until their unveiling by the Holy Spirit because up until their disclosure, they were **yet to be understood?**

Although I, as well as nearly all serious students of the Bible, have always held to the "can't-date" idea, I can no longer find any biblical basis for that belief. **A biblical prohibition to know exact dates for end-time events does not seem to exist.**

CHAPTER 16
IMMINENCE, ITS DEFINITION AND PURPOSE

Imminence—what does it mean? What is the biblical definition? What is the accepted "theological" definition?

Since most defenders of the faith present "imminence" as proof positive that God forbids our knowing exact dates of end-time events,[a] we need to examine the definition of imminence as they give it.[b] Their three-part definition goes something like this. Imminence means:

1) Jesus can come at any time,
2) the time of His appearance cannot be known, and
3) no event has ever stood between His first coming and His promised return.

Most importantly, as we read their literature, we notice that after presenting this definition for imminence, the rest of the proofs given for "why we cannot know exact dates"

---

[a] The Rapture in particular

[b] This author has been very careful throughout to refrain from naming authors or Bible teachers whose work is questioned. Specifically here, in the case of the definition of imminence an interested reader could turn to almost anyone's work on the subject of imminence, and see the same definition that is held up here for examination.

The purpose is plain. We need to examine beliefs and ideas in light of the Scripture, not single out individuals for criticism.

is built solely upon **their own** previously stated definition.

This system of proof, recognized as "circular reasoning," describes a faulty method of substantiating one's beliefs. This method can be described as people stating something to be true without proving their position and then drawing conclusions based on their original unsubstantiated statement. Let me give you an example of circular reasoning. I heard a radio teacher say, "Satan cannot perform miracles, he is just a master of deception."

A caller questioned this statement by asking, "You say Satan cannot perform miracles, yet his henchmen, the magicians of Pharaoh, were able to turn their staffs into serpents. How do you explain that?"

The teacher replied, "Since we know that Satan cannot perform miracles, he obviously used trickery." The conclusion in this case was based on his original unsubstantiated statement. Circular reasoning authenticates nothing.

We then must ask, "If the previously stated popular definition of imminence is so solid, why wouldn't a better case be presented?" The explanation for this remains elusive.

Trying to find out where this foundational, set-in-stone definition originates is difficult. (Although *Webster's Dictionary* is certainly not the final authority for determining the definition of theological terms, his work is an intelligent place to begin our search for an accurate understanding of word meanings.)

Webster defines imminence as "1. the quality or fact of being imminent: also imminency; 2. something imminent; impending evil, danger, etc." Webster's definition of imminent is "to project over, threaten...likely to happen without delay; impending; threatening; said of danger, evil, misfortune, etc."

We can easily recognize the correlation of the popular theological definition in point 1 to that of Webster, (i.e., "Jesus can come at any time" compared to "imminence means likely to happen without delay; impending"). However, points number 2 and 3 of the theological definition are conspicuously absent from Webster, (i.e., "Imminence means the time of His appearance cannot be known" and "No event has ever stood between His first coming and the promise of His return.")

In exegesis[a], we should never compose a definition for a theological word that differs from a language's standard use of that word without giving some biblical proofs for the meaning. Until we do give proof, we cannot use our own definition as validation for the original belief being true.

Oddly, this "expanded definition" of imminence itself seems to be the cornerstone of the doctrine of imminence. Additionally, for many, this doctrine is the core of the "can't-ever-know" belief.

Let us consider for a moment a different definition of imminence. It is this: Jesus will come for His bride and until or unless we know when, we must expect Him at any time.

Carefully examine **any** definition given for imminence making sure understanding of the doctrine is gleaned solely from Scripture. Imminence is biblical, but let us search out and cling to its **biblical definition**.

---

[a] Analysis or interpretation of a word

The Doctrine of Imminence

In examining the widely-held and most-revered doctrine of imminence, some interesting information surfaces. [Certainly it is imminent that Jesus will return, so only the "expanded version" of imminence is being reviewed here] Two proofs are said to carry this doctrine:

1. The Early Church held the doctrine of imminence, and

2. the Scriptures teach it.

Concerning the first point, I certainly agree that most believers throughout history have lived with expectancy. But we must also remember that for at least four thousand years mankind lived with another promised hope. They looked for a man born of woman who would defeat Satan. Of course, the Jews (in particular) lived with the imminent hope of the coming Messiah for nearly two thousand years. However, throughout that whole era of expectancy, God gave successive bits of information as to when this Messiah would arrive.

From this example we see that **until or unless we receive definite information about the time of any coming event, we live in expectancy.** However, this truth does not preclude the possibility of ever comprehending more of the information (we already have) about specific timing.

Now let us scrutinize the second reason given for this expanded definition of the doctrine of imminence: The Scriptures teach it.

After examining all the Scriptures garnered by the most ardent exponents of imminence, one truth becomes evident. All of the Scriptures given concern expectation and promise for the purpose of exhortation and encouragement.[a] **None** of these "imminence" verses refer one way or another to knowledge about when the Rapture may occur.

For example, the description of the Rapture in I Corinthians 15:52 stating that we are raised "*in the twinkling of an eye*" is used by many teachers to prove imminence. In actuality, this "twinkling of an eye" simply describes the instantaneous nature of the occurrence. Many happenings in life are quick such as the striking of a match, or the blaze of a flashbulb. Just because an incident is quick, does not necessarily mean it is unknown ahead of time.

Let me give a hometown example of imminence. If I drive over and drop my daughter off at a friend's house to play, I might say, "Honey, I'm going to run some errands and then swing back to pick you up. You be good now!" She knows I'm coming back, that I'll pick her up in the car, and that she should behave.

Now I may come back in a few minutes or a few hours. I may just drive up without warning or I might call her from my last stop and tell her, "I'll be by to pick you up in five minutes."

In the same way, when you examine each of the "imminence" verses you'll see the type of information given to us by God concerning the Rapture is similar to what I gave to my daughter about picking her up.

None of these verses state that the time could never be known. Until or unless believers receive details about the time of the Rapture, we live just knowing, "He's coming, maybe today." The expectancy taught in these verses in no

---

[a] These are the imminence verses. John 14:2-3; Acts 1:11; I Corinthians 1:7; 15:51-52; Philippians 3:20-21; Colossians 3:4; I Thessalonians 1:9-10; 4:16-17; 5:5-9; I Timothy 6:14; Titus 2:13; James 5:8-9; I Peter 3:3-4; Revelation 3:10; 22:17-22

way precludes the possibility of **ever** knowing an exact date for the Rapture.

It is astonishing to me that there are so many preachers who contradict themselves by adamantly teaching, "There are no signs which must precede the Rapture" while at the same time giving stirring sermons saying, "Just look at the signs. We are in the last days!"

I agree with those who pronounce "we should look for Jesus, not for signs!" That is exactly what this whole book is intended to promote! I am looking for Jesus but I also want to encourage believers to actively look for the time of our departure to be with Him.

Another statement that contains a seeming conflict results from the expanded definition of imminence. Often the declaration is made, "Jesus is coming back soon, but 'no man knows the day or the hour' so be ready, because you don't know when the Rapture will occur." For those who believe the Rapture and the Second Coming are two distinctly different events separated by seven years of time, why is the terminology for the two events combined as if they were the same occurrence?

In the previous chapters, the "prohibition" verses are seen to be references mostly to the Second Coming. As we have seen, the prohibition apparently applied only to believers of Jesus' day. Doesn't it seem time that the body of Christ rethink its traditional stand on the dating of end-time occurrences?

Imminence Motivates

At this point some Christians quickly speak up and say, "The imminence of Christ's return has always been a strong motivating factor in the history of the Christian Church."

That is most certainly true. From the days of the
apostles until this very day, imminence has been an
integral part of our Christian experience. However, when
some go on to suggest that, "If believers were to know the
exact date of the Rapture, they would go out and live in
wild sin until just before Jesus' coming," I most heartily
disagree. Could anyone really believe that the only reason
Christians live their lives honoring the Lord is because
they are afraid to get caught sinning when the Rapture
comes? This running-out-to-sin objection gives the
impression that all believers constantly crave a life of
wickedness, and that the Christian life of obedience is
without present reward or joy.

Certainly, at times, the thought of the imminent return
of Christ spurs us on, but for the most part our obedience
is a result of a desire to please the Lord. The thought of
imminence, as it has traditionally been interpreted from
Scripture, is definitely motivational. However, if we were
to discover that the exact date of the Rapture was to occur
in the time we were living, **that knowledge would be the
biggest spur for service yet!**

Another thought of some is, "To deny imminence is to
take the hope of His coming away from every previous
generation."[a] In considering this idea, one needs to review
God's promise of a coming redeemer to be born of a
woman.[b]

Many theologians discuss women's belief in the
imminent arrival of the redeemer when they teach about

---

[a] That some future generation would have added insight is actually mentioned
by Jesus. He prophesied that the specific future generation that would see the
beginning of the end times would also experience the coming of Jesus. Matthew
24:34

[b] Genesis 3

Eve.* Donald Barnhouse, in his book *Genesis,* explains that
Eve's statement at Cain's birth reveals her belief that this
child was the promised Messiah. Barnhouse writes, "In
Hebrew the true meaning is found. 'I have gotten a man,
even the deliverer.'"[120]

When God gave the added promise that this redeemer
would come from the womb of a Jewish mother, the
conviction of imminence continued among Jewish women.
Even though the Lord began to weave into the Old
Testament Scriptures (particularly the book of Daniel)
some details as to when this Messiah would come upon
the scene, Jewish mothers continued to hope that they
might be the chosen vessel. The motivating promise of the
imminent arrival of the Messiah was every bit real to them,
even though with hindsight we can look back today and
know that Messiah would not arrive until thousands of
years after the original promise.

In the same way believers of past generations who
have looked for the promised Rapture in their lifetimes
have been motivated by the possibility of His coming. The
prospect that some future generation (perhaps ours) might
actually know the time of the Rapture can in no way take
away the hope of these previous generations of believers.

Imminent, But Not Yet

The belief from the very beginning of the birth of the
Church was, "Jesus could come back at any time." Since
the Early Church knew only that they were to be ready
and that Jesus would come back, the climate of expectancy
existed. But the added idea that "There has never been

---

* See McGee's *Genesis,* as well as John J. Davis' *Paradise To Prison.*

any circumstance or happening that needs to occur before the Rapture could transpire" must be examined.

In considering any belief, God's Word, not the longevity of a belief, must be our guide. Upon examination of the following Scriptures, perhaps this expanded definition of imminence needs to be reassessed.

1. It is commonly understood that Jesus told Peter the type of death he would experience.[a] Although there is a difference of opinion as to whether the death Jesus foretold for Peter was martyrdom or old age, the importance of this encounter to prophetic study is that **as long as Peter was alive**, the Rapture could not occur! The fact that Peter would **die** (and therefore not be raptured) is also mentioned by Peter long after the recorded encounter in the book of John.[b]

Some disagree with this observation. They suggest that neither Peter nor the Early Church really understood the prophecy of Jesus concerning Peter's death. They suggest that since no one understood that Peter would die (rather than be raptured) before Jesus returned and since most people didn't know about the prophecy anyway,[c] the imminency[d] of the coming of Christ existed even before Peter's death.

---

[a] John 21:18-23

[b] II Peter 1:14

[c] The proof given for this idea is that the book of John, which records Jesus' prophecy, was written twenty years after Peter's death. This premise neglects the fact that the apostles and other believers verbally carried Jesus' words from town to town before His words were written in the Gospels.

[d] Remember, the imminence referred to here is the "expanded" version which says "no event has ever had to occur before the Rapture."

The problem with their objection is twofold. First: It is only an assumption to say, "No one understood the words of Christ concerning Peter's death" and second, whether or not anyone understood the words of Jesus is irrelevant. He stated that Peter would die. What could be more clear? Peter would experience death. He therefore would not be raptured alive, so the Rapture **could not occur** until Peter died.[a]

According to this information, [expanded] imminence was not in effect at least until Peter's death. Jesus' words to Peter contradict the often-repeated statement, "There is not, nor has there ever been anything that must occur before the Rapture."

2. **The Lord specifically speaks of Paul's future on earth.** Three days after Paul's conversion, God revealed that Paul will *"bear my name before the Gentiles, and kings, and the children of Israel: For I will show him how great things he must suffer for my name's sake."*[b]   Again the idea that the Rapture always could have occurred at any time fails in the light of God's words. The Rapture could not have happened until Paul witnessed to the Gentiles, kings, and the Jews, nor until Paul had "suffered great things." Since Jesus promised to take all the believers in the Rapture, including Paul, the Rapture simply could not occur until Paul fulfilled God's prophecy.

---

[a] In the pursuit of protecting the important belief of the pre-tribulation Rapture, some find themselves spread thin protecting the expanded version of imminence. Those who question any part of the expanded version are instantly suspected of promoting a post-tribulation view (meaning that Jesus will come for believers after Tribulation).

[b] Acts 9:15, 16

Watchfulness Encouraged

We are all familiar with the statement of Jesus, *"Therefore be ye also ready: for in such an hour as ye think not the Son of man cometh."*[a] Should we conclude from this statement that no Christian will ever know the time of the Rapture?

To answer this question please note that the people being reprimanded in this passage are **the ones who did not watch, and were therefore "surprised" at His arrival.** Besides, isn't this passage, as previously discussed, a discourse about the timing of **the Second Coming of Jesus, not the Rapture?**

Why do we continue to use this verse as a reason that the exact moment of the Rapture cannot be known? Could the reason for the constant misapplication of Second Coming verses to the Rapture be because this "no man can know" belief has a weak base?

There are three groups of "watch" verses that pertain to end-time events. The first group relates to watchfulness during the Tribulation to avoid judgment. These Scriptures,[b] mostly from the Olivet discourse, are seen by many such as McGee, Walvoord, and the contributors to *The Pulpit Commentary* to be definite references to the Second Coming.[121]

The second group of "watch" or "look" verses[c] tells us as New Testament believers to watch [monitor] our conduct.

---

[a] Matthew 24:42, 44

[b] Matthew 24:42-25:13; Mark 13:33-37; Luke 21:35-36 and Hebrews 9:28

[c] I Corinthians 16:13; Colossians 4:2; II Timothy 4:5

Just a few of all the "watch" and "look" verses[a] might be referring to the Rapture (as opposed to the Second Coming). If these verses refer to the Rapture, are we to believe that God is telling us to tilt our heads back so we can see Jesus when He comes for us, or is He suggesting that we be in a ready condition of holy living? Is He not also exhorting us to study and correctly interpret the Scriptures so that we will be aware of the time of His coming?

No matter which of these ideas we choose, we can be assured that those who "watch" **will not be surprised when Jesus comes!** This conclusion is strongly borne out in the Bible, "*Be watchful, and strengthen the things which remain, that are ready to die: for I have not found thy works perfect before God. Remember therefore how thou hast received and heard, and hold fast, and repent. If therefore thou shalt not watch, I will come on thee as a thief, and thou shalt not know what hour I will come upon thee.*"[b]

---

[a] I Thessalonians 5:6; Titus 2:13; I Peter 4:7

[b] Revelation 3:2, 3

CHAPTER 17
ERRONEOUS DATES

"Ah yes," some say, "don't you remember that fanatics have forever been trying to date the Rapture, and they've always been wrong?"

It's true. They have all been wrong, but that in no way is a logical proof that we should not search the Scriptures on this subject.

Many people in past history tried to fly. Onlookers laughed while those who believed in the possibility of flight tried thousands of unique methods but failed. However, the inventors persevered, and as we now know, they discovered the secrets of flight. Past failure or previous incorrect deductions concerning dates for end-time events simply does not prove that the dates can never be discovered.

The Jews have also struggled with the precarious position on "date setting." In fact, the Talmud refers to leading rabbis who were frustrated with those who tried to calculate the coming of Messiah. It seems many students were anxious to study the prophetic dates in Daniel in order to discover the time for the coming of Messiah. The rabbis harshly warned that no one would be allowed to study and set a date for the appearing of Messiah. They pronounced, "Blast the bones of the end-time calculators. For when they say such-and-such time and it does not come, the people despair and say: 'It's never going to come'."[122]

They indicate that the avoidance of studying specific dates grew out of a desire to shield their followers from possible disappointment. The importance they placed on never making a mistake influenced these leaders to avoid the study of the prophetic Scriptures God had provided concerning the coming Messiah! I wonder if they ever questioned why the Lord had incorporated these dates in the Scriptures?

How tragic! If the Jews had counted the days given to them in the book of Daniel, they could have welcomed Jesus into the city on the day of His triumphal entry.

That Scripture in Daniel states, *"From the going forth of the commandment to restore and build Jerusalem unto the Messiah the Prince shall be seven weeks, and threescore and two weeks...and after threescore and two weeks shall Messiah be cut off."*[a]

J. Vernon McGee writes in his book *Daniel* concerning an Old Testament prophecy telling of the coming Messiah, "I feel that the decree of Artaxerxes in the twentieth year of his reign (Nehemiah 2:1-8) meets the requirements of Daniel 9:25. The commandment to rebuild the city of Jerusalem was issued in the month Nisan 445 B.C. That then will be our starting point.

"The first seven weeks of forty-nine years bring us to 397 B.C. and to Malachi and the end of the Old Testament. These were 'troublous times,' as witnessed to by both Nehemiah and Malachi.

"Sixty-two weeks, or 434 years, bring us to the Messiah... On this day Jesus rode into Jerusalem, offering

---

[a] Daniel 9:25, 26

Himself for the first time, publicly and officially, as the Messiah."[123]

Evidently, from the words of Jesus, if anyone had desired to understand that prophecy in Daniel, they could have. Just after His triumphal entry on Palm Sunday, Jesus looked over the city of Jerusalem and *"wept over it, saying, If thou hadst known, even thou, at least in this thy day, the things which belong unto thy peace! but now they are hid from thine eyes."*[a] (Remember earlier Jesus explained why the meaning of His words were hidden from most people. He said, *"This people's heart is grown cold, and their ears are dull of hearing, and their eyes they have closed."*[b] Jesus finishes his indictment after Palm Sunday by describing the reason for the national destruction to come, *"Because thou knewest not the time of thy visitation."*[c] Regrettably, the Jews chose not to study a portion of the Scriptures in order to insure their own credibility!

Even sadder yet, I hear those same words echoed today. "What if we are wrong? What if we calculate the wrong date? Nobody would believe us any more. We cannot afford to lose our credibility, you know." It appears at times that the fear of proposing an incorrect date has canceled out the study of God's intricately-woven prophetic time patterns in the Bible.

How amazing! This mentality still exists today. We in the twentieth century still seem more concerned with what people think of us than with pursuing God-given information. Are we wise in choosing not to study

---

[a] Luke 13:41, 42

[b] Matthew 13:15

[c] Luke 19:42, 44

portions of God's Word that might reveal the time of the soon coming Rapture?

Who Do You Trust?

You may be one who stiffens at the very mention of "date setting." Your major anxiety in connection with anyone choosing an exact date for the Rapture and the coming end-time events is, "What if the date is wrong? Think of all the people who will be disillusioned and lose faith."

Let's address this question head-on. If you or anyone else reads and **automatically believes** any prophetic information, you are destined for disappointment. God cautions everyone to examine instruction received. We must hold all incoming teaching up to the light of His written Word to determine *"whether these things are so."*[a] Jesus promised that the Holy Spirit would be the ultimate teacher of those who trust God. This honor and this responsibility must never be given to any human instructor. Jesus promised that the Holy Spirit would *"guide you into all truth...and he will show you things to come."*[b]

As long as people place their faith in Jesus Christ and the Word of God, they will never have occasion to "lose faith." However, when anyone trusts a human leader for ultimate truth, disappointment is the inevitable result.

An often voiced objection to searching for exact information on the timing of biblically forecast events is, "I don't think it's right for Christians to look into the future. Doesn't that show lack of faith?"

---

[a] Acts 17:11

[b] John 16:13

This belief is incongruous when compared to the lives of the questioners. Most people think nothing of listening to the weatherman's forecast for the coming day or studying the predictions of economists when planning their investments. The gathering of military intelligence is a custom that dates back to Bible times, and going to a doctor for check-ups is considered wise. These experts we consult may or may not be accurate, yet we listen in order to learn as much as we can from them. In all of these searches for clues to the future, we feel no shame in seeking to obtain precise information about the future, nor are we unduly surprised if their projections aren't 100 percent accurate.

Stockbrokers, doctors, weathermen, and military agents are rewarded for their attempts at determining the future but the religious community pounces upon those who try to understand and apply the prophetic portions of the Bible. Again, this practice is incongruous and stifles much exciting study of Scripture.

Why is it that we treat explorations into the timing of future events so differently? The Bible is the only sure source of knowledge about the future. How strange that we choose to shrug off God's words concerning the future and instead rely on secular forecasters. This attitude is amazing. **The greatest event scheduled for the inhabitants of planet earth may soon transpire,** yet we fail to dig into the Bible to discover its timing. Sometimes it seems people are either afraid to know when the Rapture might happen or they are simply uninterested in God's program for the future.

When predictors of antiquity tried and failed to come up with a correct date for end-time events, many in the religious world reacted in horror. Why did they react in horror? Did they believe the followers of God to be so fragile that they could not survive the passing of an incorrectly projected date?

Of course we must be cautious. We must notice the difference between those who project possibilities and those who want you to trust their "inside-message" from God. History records a number of self-appointed gurus who have claimed special revelations from God about the date of Jesus' coming. Again and again, followers of these self-appointed, enlightened ones have been bitterly disappointed. Those leaders were wrong to have claimed that "God told them a date." (God evidently did not tell them since Jesus has not yet come.)

Again, our ultimate trust must be in God, not human leaders. If information given to us (from anyone) cannot be verified in the Scripture, we must not count it as a message from God. Most importantly, we must each take personal responsibility for our own beliefs.

Another area that deserves examination is in the arena of prophetic teaching. Certainly, God desires those who are Christians to understand and speak with authority on matters of doctrine. However, when it comes to teaching prophetic information, all of us need to exercise some caution. Our exposition of prophetic themes is often presented with such authority. Isn't there a difference between what we "know" the Bible teaches and what we "think" will transpire in the future? Many major prophetic occurrences are plainly described in Scripture, but other future events are not as easily defined. A few "probablys" and "likelys" would be a breath of fresh air in prophetic presentations.

The presumption that feast days represent future prophetic events has strong proof behind it. Still, some of the observations may be wrong. As the time for the Rapture draws closer, information should continue to amass until conditional words no longer need to be used. Until that time, continue to study the Bible and look for Jesus.

Remember, **God is a date setter.** As we've seen throughout the whole Bible, both in the spirit and the letter, God reveals His plans for the future. Unfortunately, most of the time, most of the people have missed this prophetic information. Sometimes they missed by purposely disregarding God's warnings. In fact, repeatedly in the Old Testament, we see instances where God's message concerning the future was ignored. This disregard for God's words concerning the future can be seen in the lives of individuals, families, religious and national leaders, entire nations, and mankind as a whole.

When God imparted prophetic information, He spoke both of impending judgment and potential rescue. He referred to those who heard these warnings as either "awake" or "asleep." Often these messages were sent to people who professed to be following God, but who refused to respond to the specific words of God. They were asleep.

Remember, at the time of Jesus' birth, abundant information had been given to the Jews about when Messiah would arrive, yet nearly everyone living was unaware of His arrival. God states in the Bible that when the Wise Men came to Jerusalem searching for Jesus, Herod *"was troubled and all Jerusalem with him."*[a]

We all have a choice. We can become "troubled" at the thought of looking for exact prophetic times, or we can be "wise" and follow the biblical signs to look for the timing of future events.

---

[a] Matthew 2:1-3

How much will God allow mankind to know about the timing of end-time events? The information in this book is written to encourage you to see that God does reveal future events to His children who wish to know it. Scripture leads us to believe that Abraham had asked God about the future. Jesus' comment on this subject was, *"Abraham rejoiced to see my day: and he saw it, and was glad."*[a]

Today, we also have the option to rejoice by looking at biblical information concerning things to come. The warning contained in Revelation 3:3 might apply to this dilemma of whether or not to look into the future. *"Remember therefore how thou hast received and heard, and hold fast, and repent. If therefore thou shalt **not watch**, I will come on thee as a thief, and thou shalt not know what hour I will come upon thee."*

Jesus is telling us here that we are **to know** the hour of His coming.

How Then Should We Live

I now believe, as many others do, that there is no scriptural prohibition to look for the date of the Rapture. As the true Rapture date draws near, I believe that all students of the Word will see more clearly.

For now I have found, as a Christian, that the study of end-time prophesies causes me to apply more meaningfully the words of Ephesians 5:16, *"redeeming the time, because the days are evil."*

---

[a] John 8:56

The scriptural study of prophecy makes real the words of God, *"Looking for that blessed hope, and the glorious appearing of the great God and our Savior Jesus Christ."*[a]

---

[a] Titus 2:13

CONCLUSION
IS PROPHECY A WASTE OF TIME?

Some Christians, after considering the possibility of **knowing** the actual date of the Rapture, respond, "Why should I waste my time on studying prophecy or looking for some specific date? My concern is winning souls and living a godly life. Knowing an exact date wouldn't change my lifestyle so why take the time?"

Giving these dedicated believers the benefit of the doubt, let us agree they are actually living every day of their life as if Jesus might come that very day. (Truthfully I have not met an abundance of this kind of Christian.) Still, most believers I know have many long-term plans that would not be in effect if they actually **knew** a close date that Jesus was going to come for them.

Certainly, if we do not have a definite date, we need both long and short-term plans. However, no matter how dedicated we might be, if we were to see a definite date outlined in the Bible, then surely the tempo and choices in our lives would be affected.

Becoming engaged is a momentous event. "Someday," the happy couple beams, "we will be getting married." When, however, the date is set, the intensity, the fervor, the aim of each day's schedule is affected by the upcoming date of the marriage. So, too, those who plan someday to meet Jesus and go to heaven are happy about their future. But discovering a possible date for this "out-of-this-world" experience is bound to produce an increased excitement for service and dedication to God.

More reason than that, however, is that we must be very careful in stating what we **will** or **will not** study in the Scriptures. How bold it is of us to decide not to study certain biblical subjects saying, "It won't affect my lifestyle so why bother?" If we are not prohibited from searching the Scriptures for exact dates, and if those dates are there, they were put there by God himself. They were put there for us. They were put there to study. They were put there to discover at the appointed time.

Alas, as with many new thoughts, some readers will probably react with, "I can't give you an exact Scripture, but I still believe you can't know," or, "Sure, I can see it's not prohibited to date the Rapture, but knowing the exact date just doesn't interest me."

The excitement of studying God's Word concerning prophetic timing is frustratingly difficult to share. No one enjoys the possibility of being branded as a "date setter" by fellow believers. It would be much easier to tuck these questions and observations into an obscure place and continue with the majority's approach to this subject.

We must all remember that God's Word warns, "*There shall come in the last days scoffers, walking after their own lusts, And saying, Where is the promise of his coming?*" These people are said to be "*willingly ignorant.*"[a] We recognize today that these scoffers are not just unbelievers. Some are Christians who are so busy building their kingdoms on earth that they have ceased looking for Jesus.

---

[a] II Peter 3:3-5

My heart's desire is to serve the Lord and honor Him by believing sound doctrine. This information is prepared for the body of Christ to ponder and critique. With great sincerity, my hope is that either the error of these observations will be **scripturally** rejected, or that these thoughts will excite others to further study along these lines.

What is your belief concerning the applications of Scripture in this book?

When Is The Rapture?

After you worked your way through all this information, you didn't yet find a positive date for the Rapture, did you? That is because I still do not know the date. Certainly there is strong evidence from the Jewish Feasts for the Rapture to occur on some Rosh HaShanah, but we don't yet know the year.

The stage is set. The players in the Middle East and around the world are taking their places, and the house lights have started to dim. We only await God's opening of the curtain to begin His final act of the "Times of the Gentiles." Can it be much longer?

Every year toward the end of summer, as Rosh HaShanah draws close, my excitement mounts. Every year after Rosh HaShanah, when the believers have not been summoned, I take a deep breath and say, "Lord, I had hoped to be with You right now but it appears there is work yet to be done." As the years pass, I'm learning what the Apostle Paul meant when he wrote, "*For I am in a straight between two, having a desire to depart, and to be with*

Christ; which is far better: Nevertheless to abide in the flesh is more needful for you."[a]

Jesus **is** coming. He will come **according to God's divine plan.** Until He does come for us, we must continue to study the prophetic Scriptures. For now, be encouraged to walk with God and continue to watch for Jesus by living out this promise of God. *"I have fought a good fight, I have finished my course, I have kept the faith: Henceforth there is laid up for me a crown of righteousness, which the Lord, the righteous judge, shall give me at that day: and not to me only, but **unto all them also that love his appearing.**"*[b]

As we wait, I hope after reading, studying, and praying about the information in this book you, too, will feel that the prohibition "to know" **does not exist.** When many believers begin to prayerfully search the Scriptures, I believe God will be true to His promise in John 16:13, *"Howbeit when he, the Spirit of truth, is come, he will guide you into all truth: for he shall not speak of himself; but whatsoever he shall hear, that shall he speak: **and he will show you things to come.**"*

---

[a] Philippians 1:23, 24

[b] II Timothy 4:7-8

GLOSSARY

Hebrew words are denoted by an asterisk. Hebrew months are denoted by double asterisks.

Months are listed using the original order as given by God placing Abib (Nisan) as the first month.

Since the letters of the Hebrew alphabet are unique to their language, English versions of Hebrew words often are seen with more than one spelling.

Abib**	Original name of the first Hebrew calendar month Nisan.
Adar**	Twelfth month of the Hebrew calendar.
Antichrist	Satan-led man who will govern the world during a future seven-year period.
apostasy	A falling away from godly truth into gross error.
Aaron	Brother of Moses and chosen by God to be the first high priest. All priests came from his descendants.
Av**	Fifth month of the Hebrew calendar.
Azazel*	The Yom Kippur goat upon whose head the sins of the Jewish nation were placed.
Bikkurim*	Hebrew for Firstfruits which is also the celebration day of Jesus' Resurrection.
Chinuch*	Hebrew commentary of the Bible.
Church Age	Theological term for the expanse of time from the Day of Pentecost to the Rapture.
Elul**	Sixth month of the Hebrew calendar.
Erev Yom Kippur*	The evening before the actual day of Yom Kippur.
exegesis	A critical explanation of a portion of Scripture.

Gedaliah* (fast of)	A fast held on the third day of Tishri beginning the "Days of Awe."
Gentile	Any person who is not a Jew.
Gregorian Calendar	An A.D. 1582 adaptation of the calendar which had been introduced by Julius Caesar in 46 B.C. (Julian Calendar).
Hag-Ha Matzot*	Feast of Unleavened Bread which begins with the partaking of the Passover meal on Nisan 15.
Hallel*	Praise, especially referring to Psalms 113–118.
Heshvan**	Eighth month of the Hebrew calendar.
high priest	Jewish priest appointed as head of all the priests. He represented the nation during the annual entrance into the Holy of Holies.
homiletics	The art of preaching.
Holy of Holies	The inner room of the Tabernacle (and later the Temple). It was 10 x 10 x 10 cubits (a cube-shaped room of about fifteen foot depth, width, and height). It contained only the Ark of the Covenant. No one entered this windowless chamber except for the high priest on the Day of Atonement (Yom Kippur).
Huppah*	Final half of the wedding ceremony so named from the "huppah" canopy under which the bride and groom stand to be married by the rabbi.
Incarnation	A theological term referring to the appearance of God in the body of a man (Jesus Christ).
Imminence	A theological term for the "at any moment" expected calling-up of the Church by Jesus Christ.
Iyar**	Second month of the Hebrew calendar.
Kislev**	Ninth year of the Hebrew calendar.

Kohen*	A priest. (All must be male descendants of the priestly line of Aaron.)
Levi*	One of Jacob's twelve sons. His descendants were called the "priestly" tribe and from them came Aaron.
liturgy	The public rites and services of the Christian church.
matzah*	Flat bread, baked without any leaven. Used during the Feast of Unleavened Bread.
matzot*	The plural of matzah.
Messiah*	The promised Redeemer.
messianic*	Having to do with the Messiah.
Millennium	Theological term for the thousand-year time of peace yet to come in the future (Zechariah 14:9-21; Revelation 20:1-7).
Nisan**	First month of the Hebrew calendar. This is the religious calendar order as originally given by God.
Paschal*	Pertaining to Passover.
Pentecost	Feast of Weeks (the fiftieth day after Firstfruits or Resurrection).
Pesach*	Passover.
priest	One who officiates from man to God. In Judaism he must be a man from the tribe of Levi and a descendant of Aaron.
rabbi*	A teacher of the Jewish religion.
Rapture	The snatching away of believers by Jesus Christ.
Rosh HaShanah*	Feast of the Trumpets celebrated on Tishri 1.
Sabbath	The seventh day of the Jewish week counted from sundown to sundown. Corresponds to the Gentile's Friday night and Saturday day. "Sabbos" is the spelling used by most Jews.

Second Coming	The bodily return of Jesus Christ.
Seder*	The ceremony (or dinner) of the Passover meal which is eaten on the evening of Nisan 15.
Shabbat*	The Sabbath before the Day of Atonement.
Shuvah Shavuot*	Feast of the fiftieth day after Firstfruits, also known as Pentecost.
Shiddukhin*	The arrangements and announcement of an engagement for marriage.
shofar*	A trumpet which is usually made from a ram's horn and sometimes from another clean animal's horn but never from metal.
Silvan**	Third month of the Hebrew calendar.
Succoth*	Feast of the Tabernacles or Booths which begins on Tishri 15.
Tabernacle	Tent for sacrificial observances, designed by God and built during Moses' time.
Tabernacles	Referring to the week long feast of Succoth which begins on Tishri 15.
Talmud*	Jewish commentaries on the Tanakh or Old Testament.
Tamuz**	Fourth month of the Jewish calendar.
Temple	First permanent worship structure built in Jerusalem for sacrificial observances. This Temple, built by Solomon in 1004 B.C., was pillaged and left in disrepair by 640 B.C. It was gradually rebuilt and used until Herod began his grandiose version of the Temple in 19 B.C. The Romans completely leveled his Temple in A.D. 70, and no Temple has been built on the site since then.
Tevet**	Tenth month of the Hebrew calendar.
Tishri**	Seventh month of the Hebrew calendar.

Torah*	The first five books of the Hebrew Bible. This term is often used when referring to the whole Jewish Bible (Old Testament).
Tribulation	A biblical term for the seven-year period of severe judgment from God upon the unbelieving population of the earth. This time begins with a pseudo peace led by the Antichrist, but ends in the worst time of judgment the world has ever known.
Yom Kippur*	Feast called the Day of Atonement, held on Tishri 10.
Yom Teruah*	Day of Sounding the Horn; biblical name for Rosh HaShanah from Numbers 29:1.

BIBLIOGRAPHY

Agnon, S.Y. *Days of Awe*. New York: Schocken Books, 1948.

Alnor, William M. *Soothsayers of the Second Advent*. Old Tappan, NJ: Power Books, Fleming Revell Co., 1989.

Barnhouse, Donald Grey. *Genesis*. Grand Rapids, MI: Zondervan Publishing House, 1970.

Berry, George Ricker. *Interlinear Greek — English New Testament*. Grand Rapids, MI: Baker Book House, 1987, 1989.

Bloch, Abraham P. *The Biblical and Historical Background of the Jewish Holy Days*. New York: KTAV Publishing House, Inc., 1978.

Buksbazen, Victor. *The Gospel in the Feasts of Israel*. Fort Washington, PA: Christian Literature Crusade, Inc., 1954.

Burgess, Edward. *Christ: The Crown of the Torah*. Grand Rapids, MI: Zondervan Publishing House, 1986.

Church, J.R. *The High Holy Days*. Oklahoma City: Southwest Radio Church, 1980.

Civelli, Joseph. *The Messiah's Return*. Nashville, TN: World Bible Society, 1988.

Daniel, Carey L. *The Bible's Seeming Contradictions*. Grand Rapids, MI: Zondervan Publishing House, 1941.

Davis, John J. *Paradise to Prison*. Grand Rapids, MI: Baker Book House, 1975.

Davis, Leonard J. *Myths and Facts*. Washington, DC: Near East Report, 1989.

Deal, Colin. *The Day and the Hour Jesus Will Return*. Nashville, TN: World Bible Society, 1989.

Edersheim, Alfred. *The Life and Times of Jesus the Messiah*. Peabody, MA: Hendrickson Publishers, 1883.

Encyclopedia Judaica. Jerusalem: Keter Publishing House, 1972.

Evans, Mike. *Israel: America's Key To Survival*. Bedford, TX: Bedford Books, 1983.

Freeman, James M. *Manners and Customs of the Bible*. Plainfield, NJ: Logos International, 1972.

Fruchtenbaum, Arnold G., *The Feast of Passover 1986, The Feast of Channukah 1987* Tustin, CA: Ariel Ministries.

Fuchs, Daniel. *Israel's Holy Days in Type and Prophecy.* Neptune, NJ: Loizeaux Brothers, 1985.

Gaebelein, Arno C. *The Gospel of Matthew.* Neptune, NJ: Loizeaux Brothers, 1961.

Gaster, Theodor. *Festivals of the Jewish New Year.* New York: William Morrow & Co., 1952.

Glaser, Mitch and Zhava. *The Fall Feasts of Israel.* Chicago: Moody Press, 1987.

Good, Joseph. *Rosh HaShanah and the Messianic Kingdom to Come.* Port Arthur, TX: Hatikva Ministries, 1989.

Goodman, Philip. *The Passover Anthology.* Philadelphia: The Jewish Publication Society of America, 1961.

Goodman, Philip. *The Rosh HaShanah Anthology.* Philadelphia: The Jewish Publication Society of America, 1970.

Goodman, Philip. *The Shavuot Anthology.* Philadelphia: The Jewish Publication Society of America, 1974.

Goodman, Philip. *The Sukkot/Simhat Torah Anthology.* Philadelphia: The Jewish Publication Society of America, 1988.

Goodman, Philip. *The Yom Kippur Anthology.* Philadephia: The Jewish Publication Society of America, 1971.

Gross, David C. *The Jewish People's Almanac.* New York: Hippocrene Books, 1988.

Habershon, Ada R. *Types in the Old Testament.* Grand Rapids, MI: Kregel Publications, 1988.

Harevueni, Nogah. *Nature in Our Biblical Heritage.* Kiryat Ono, Israel: Neot Kedumim Ltd.

Henry, Matthew. *Commentaries of Genesis to Deuteronomy and Matthew to John.* Old Tappan, NJ: Fleming H. Revell Co.

The Holy Bible: Authorized King James Version. Nashville: Thomas Nelson, Inc., 1976.

Ironside, Harry A. *Matthew*. Neptune, NJ: Loizeaux Brothers, 1948.

Israel My Glory. Vol. 48. No. 3. Bellmawr, NJ: The Friends of Israel Gospel Ministry, Inc., 1990.

Jeffrey, Grant R. *Armageddon Appointment With Destiny*. Toronto, Ontario: Frontier Research Publications, 1988.

Jeffrey, Grant R. *Heaven: The Last Frontier*. Toronto, Ontario: Frontier Research Publications, 1990.

The Jewish Publication Society. *Tanakh* The New JPS Translation. Philadelphia: 1988.

Jones, Vendyl. *The Search for the Ashes of the Red Heifer*. Oklahoma City: Southwest Radio Church, 1981.

Josephus, The Works of. Peabody, MA: Hendrickson Publishers, 1987.

Kac, Arthur W. *The Messiahship of Jesus*. Grand Rapids, MI: Baker Book House, 1980.

Kac, Arthur W. *The Messianic Hope*. Grand Rapids, MI: Baker Book House, 1974.

Kieval, Herman. *The High Holy Days: Book One: Rosh Hashanah*. New York: The Burning Bush Press, 1959.

Lang, John Peter. *Commentary on the Holy Scriptures: Exodus and Leviticus*. Grand Rapids, MI: Zondervan Publishing Company.

Leibowitz, Nehama. *Studies in Bramidbar Numbers*. Jerusalem: World Zionist Organization, 1980.

Lewis, David Allen. *Prophecy 2000*. Green Forest, AR: New Leaf Press, 1990.

Lindsey, Hal. *The Late Great Planet Earth*. Grand Rapids, MI: Zondervan Publishing House, 1970.

Lindsey, Hal. *The Road to Holocaust*. New York: Bantam Books, 1989.

Lippel. *The Book of Feasts in the Holy Land Israel*. Jerusalem: Institute Of Interreligious Relations and Research, 1982.

Litvin, Danny. *Pentecost Is Jewish*. Orange, CA: Promise Publishing, 1987.

McGee, J. Vernon. *Daniel 1978, Exodus 1975, Ezra, Nehemiah & Esther 1977, Leviticus 1975, Matthew 1973, Mark 1975, Luke 1975, John 1976, Hebrews 1978.* Pasadena, CA: Thru The Bible Radio.

McGee, J. Vernon. *The Tabernacle: God's Portrait of Christ.* Pasadena, CA: Thru the Bible Radio, 1970.

Ministry of Foreign Affairs. *Facts About Israel.* Jerusalem: Information Division, 1979.

Neusner, Jacob. *Invitation to The Midrash.* San Francisco: Harper and Row, 1989.

Neusner, Jacob. *Invitation to The Talmud.* San Francisco: Harper and Row, 1973.

Pentecost, Dwight J. *Things to Come.* Grand Rapids, MI: Zondervan Publishing House, 1978.

Pettingill, William L. *Bible Questions Answered.* Grand Rapids, MI: Zondervan Publishing House, 1965.

Pink, Arthur W. *Gleanings in Exodus.* Chicago: Moody Press, 1972.

Pink, Arthur W. *Gleanings in Genesis.* Chicago: Moody Press, 1979

Price Stanley. *The Giants of Noah's Day.* Oklahoma City, OK: Southwest Radio Church, 1988

Pulpit Commentary, The. Peabody, MA: Hendrickson Publishers.

Rausch, David A. *Building Bridges.* Chicago: Moody Press, 1988.

Rosen, Ceil and Moishe. *Christ in the Passover.* Chicago: Moody Press, 1978.

Shepherd, Coulson. *Jewish Holy Days.* Neptune, NJ: Loizeaux Brothers, 1961.

Showers, Reginald E. *Behold the Bridegroom Comes.* Bellmawr, NJ: The Friends of Israel Gospel Ministry.

Spence, Very Rev. H. D. M. and Rev. Joseph S. Exell. *The Pulpit Commentary: Exodus Vols I and II.* New York: Funk and Wagnalls Company.

Steinberg, Milton. *Basic Judaism.* New York: Harvest/HBJ Book.

Strauss, Lehman. *God's Prophetic Calendar.* Neptune, NJ: Loizeaux Brothers, 1987.

Taylor, Charles R. *Get All Excited Jesus Is Coming Soon!* Redondo Beach, CA: Today in Bible Prophecy, 1974.

Taylor, Charles R. *Watch World Events*. Nashville: World Bible Society, 1989.

Stern, David H. *Jewish New Testament*. Jerusalem: Jewish New Testament Publications, 1989.

Walvoord, John F. *Matthew—Thy Kingdom Come*. Chicago: Moody Press, 1974.

Walvoord, John F. *The Rapture Question*. Grand Rapids, MI: Zondervan Publishing House, 1979.

Walvoord, John F. *The Revelation of Jesus Christ*. Chicago: Moody Press, 1966.

Waskow, Arthur. *Seasons of Our Joy*. New York: Bantam Books, 1982.

Werblowsky, R.J., Zwi and Geoffrey W. Goder, eds. *Encyclopedia of the Jewish Religion*. Israel: Massada PGC Press LTD, 1965.

Wiersbe, Warren W. *Be God's Guest: Feasts of Leviticus 23.* Lincoln, NE: Back to the Bible Broadcast, Victor Books, 1982.

Wolpin, Rabbi Nisson, ed. *Seasons of the Soul*. Agudath, Israel: Mesorah Publications Ltd., 1981.

ENDNOTES

1. William A. Alnor, *Soothsayers of the Second Advent* (Old Tappan, NJ: Power Books, Fleming Revell Co., 1989), p. 58.

2. Mircea Eliade, ed., *The Encyclopedia of Religion* (New York: MacMillan Publishing Co. 1987), vol. 9., p. 530.

3. John Elson, "Essay" *Time* (February 11, 1991), p. 88.

4. Jeffery L. Sheler, "A Revelation in the Middle East" *US News and World Report* (November 19, 1990), pp. 67-68.

5. James Hastings, ed., *The Encyclopedia of Religion and Ethics* (New York: Charles Scribner's Son), vol. 11., p. 284.

6. Ibid. vol. 11., p. 285.

7. Ron Rhodes, "Millennial Madness" *Christian Research Journal* (Fall 1990), p. 39.

8. Hastings, op. cit. pp. 285-286.

9. *L'Accomplissement des propheties, ou la deliverance prechaine de l'eglise* (Rotterdam 1686), 2 vols.

10. Hastings, op. cit. p. 286.

11. David Allen Lewis, *Prophecy 2000* (Green Forest, AR: New Leaf Press, 1990), p. 222.

12. Grant Jeffrey, *Heaven: The Last Frontier* (Toronto, Ontario:Frontier Research Publications, 1990), pp. 93-118.

13. *Jerusalem Post* (September 1, 1990).

14. "Spotlight" (*Jerusalem Post*, March 9, 1991).

15. *Encyclopedia Judaica* (Jerusalem: Keter Publishing House, 1972), vol. 11., p. 1031.

16. Ibid.

17. James M. Freeman, *Manners and Customs of the Bible* (Plainfield, NJ: Logos, 1972), p. 330.

18. *Encyclopedia Judaica* vol. 11., op. cit. p. 1031.

19. Freeman, op. cit. p. 376.

20. Charles F. Pfeiffer, Howard F. Vos and John Rea, *The Wycliffe Bible Encyclopedia* (Chicago: Moody Press 1975), p. 1082.

21. *Encyclopedia Judaica* vol. 11., op. cit. p. 1034.

22. George E. Ladd, *The Blessed Hope* pp. 99–102.

23. Coulson Shepherd, *Jewish Holy Days* (Neptune, NJ: Loizeaux Brothers 1961) p. 11.

24. Exodus 12:2, Leviticus 23:4, 5

25. Interestingly each plague demonstrated God's supremacy over the chief deities of Egypt. *See* J. Vernon McGee's opening notes for Exodus in his *Thru the Bible* version of the Bible for a detailed account of Egypt's defeated gods.

26. Abraham P. Bloch, *The Biblical and Historical Background of The Jewish Holy Days* (NY: KTAV Publishing House Ltd, 1978), p. 107.

27. Edward Burgess, *Christ: The Crown of the Torah* (Grand Rapids, MI: Zondervan Publishing House, 1986), pp. 88-89.

28. Josephus, *The Works of Josephus* "Wars of the Jews" (Peabody, MA: Hendrickson Publishers, Inc., 1987), Book 6/ Chapter 9/3.

29. Arthur W. Pink, *Gleanings in Genesis* (Chicago: Moody Press, 1978), pp. 170-171.

30. Lehman Strauss, *God's Prophetic Calendar* (Neptune, NJ: Loizeaux Brothers, 1987), pp. 28-29.

31. J. D. Douglas, ed., *The New Bible Dictionary* (Grand Rapids MI: Wm. B. Eerdmans Publishing Co., 1962), pp. 1209-1210.

32. J. Vernon McGee, *Exodus* (Pasadena, CA: Thru The Bible Radio, 1975), vol. I., pp. 99-100.
Pink, *Gleanings in Exodus* op. cit. p. 90.

33. Bloch, op. cit. p. 103.

34. Alfred Edersheim, *The Life and Times of Jesus the Messiah* (Peabody, MA: Hendrickson Publishers, 1883), p. 490.
    Encyclopedia Judaica vol. 13., op. cit. p. 170.

35. Ibid. vol. 12., op. cit. p. 22.

36. Ibid. vol. 14 p. 611.

37. Ibid. vol. 14., p. 613.

38. ibid. vol. 13., p. 171.

39. Josephus, loc. cit.

40. Pink, op. cit. p. 93.

41. Bloch, op. cit. pp. 108-109.

42. Bloch, op. cit. p.106.

43. Bloch, op. cit. p.112.

44. Bloch, op. cit. pp. 136, 137.

45. Arnold G. Fruchtenbaum, *The Feast of Passover* (Tustin, CA: Ariel Ministries, 1986) p. 7.

46. Bloch, op. cit. p. 113.

47. Douglas *The New Bible Dictionary* op. cit., pp.1140, 1141.

48. Daniel Fuchs, *Israel's Holy Days in Type and Prophecy* (Neptune, NJ: Loizeaux Brothers, 1985), p. 29.

49. *Encyclopedia Judaica* vol. 14., op. cit. p. 1319.
    Zwi R. J. Werblowsky and Geoffrey Wigoder, ed. *Encyclopedia of Jewish Religion* (Masada PEC Press Ltd., 1965), p. 401.

50. Victor Buksbazen, *The Gospel in the Feasts of Israel* (Fort Washington, PA: Christian Literature Crusade, 1954), p. 18.

51. *The Scofield Reference Bible* (Oxford University Press Inc. 1909), p. 156.

52. Bloch, op. cit. p. 185.

53. Bloch, op. cit. p. 188.
    Danny Litvin, *Pentecost Is Jewish* (Orange, CA: Promise Publishing, 1987), pp. 14-15.

54. Litvin, loc. cit.

55. Ibid. pp. 44-48.

56. Jeremiah 5:24; Hosea 5:12-6:3; Joel 2:23; Zechariah 10:1; James 5:7,8

57. Bloch, op. cit. p. 196.

58. Ibid.

59. *Encyclopedia Judaica* vol. 14., op. cit. p. 1444.

60. Theodor Gaster, *Festivals of the Jewish Year* (William Morrow & Co., 1952), p. 113.
    Herman Kieval, *The High Holy Days: Book One: Rosh Hashanah* (New York: The Burning Bush Press, 1959), p. 120.

61. Isaac Klein, *A Guide To Jewish Practices* (New York: The Jewish Theological Seminary of America, 1979), p. 196.

62. Joseph Civelli, *The Messiah's Return* (Nashville: World Bible Society, 1983), p. 37.

63. S. Y. Agnon, *Days Of Awe* (New York: Schoken Books, 1948), pp. 79-80.

64. op.cit. p. 109.

65. Bloch, op. cit. p. 25.

66. Joseph Good, *"The Akeida - Binding of the Sacrifice"* Tape series. (Port Arthur, TX: Hatikva Ministries), series st 4.

67. Bloch, op. cit. p. 21.

68. Rabbi Ishmael (second century) quoted in Bloch, op. cit. pp. 23-24.

69. Bloch, op. cit. p. 24.

70. Buksbazen, op. cit. p.25.

71. Scofield Reference Bible, 1909 edition, "The Feast of Trumpets", Leviticus 23: 23-25, note # 2, p. 157.

72. *Jerusalem Post*/March 16 1991/ p.1.

73. Bloch, op. cit. p.16.

74. Ibid. p. 24.

75. *Encyclopedia Judaica* vol. 5., op. cit. p. 1382.

76. Buksbazen, op. cit. p. 41.

77. Bloch, op.cit. p. 34.

78. Ibid. p. 34.

79. Ibid. p. 37.

80. Buksbazen, op. cit. p. 36.

81. Agnon, op. cit. p. 148.

82. J. Vernon McGee, *The Tabernacle: God's Portrait of Christ* (Pasadena, CA: Thru The Bible Radio, 1970), p. 81.

83. Burgess, op. cit. p. 107.
    Gaster, op. cit. pp. 146-147.

84. J. Vernon McGee *The Tabernacle: God's Portrait of Christ*, op.cit. p. 75.

85. *Encyclopedia Judaica* vol. 15., op. cit p. 969.

86. Ibid. vol. 15., p. 978.

87. Agnon, op. cit. p.130.

88. Ibid.

89. Philip Goodman, *The Yom Kippur Anthology* (quote from Franz Rosenzweig) (Philadelphia: The Jewish Publication Society of America, 1971), pp. 133-134.

90. Arthur Wascow, *Seasons of Our Joy* (New York: Bantam Books, 1982), p. 27.

91. From instructions in Numbers 29:12-39, each day two rams, fourteen lambs, and one goat were offered. Interestingly, the first day thirteen young bullocks (bulls) were required and each day thereafter this number diminished by one.
    According to Arthur Wascow in *Seasons of Our Joy* p. 54, "The total number of seventy bullocks being offered was said by Rabbinic tradition to celebrate the seventy nations on earth...Thus during Succoth the people of Israel became priests on behalf of all the peoples without their consent — that they needed the help of the God of Heaven." (The number of seventy for the nations comes from Genesis chapter 10.)

92. Waskow, op. cit. p. 49-52.
    Gaster, op. cit. pp. 80-83

93. Rabbi Ralph Pelcovitz, "Seasons of the Soul" (article) (Brooklyn, NY: Mesorah Publications, Ltd., 1969), p. 73.

94. Pelcovitz, ibid.

95. Gaster, op. cit. p. 86.

96. Philip Goodman, *The Sukkot/Simhat Torah Anthology* (Philadelphia: The Jewish Publication Society of America, 1988), p. 43.

97. Arno C. Gaebelein, *Concise Commentary on the Whole Bible* (Neptune, NJ:Loizeaux Brothers), p. 21.

98. Pink, *Gleanings in Genesis*, op. cit., p. 42.

99. J. Vernon McGee, *Ezra, Nehemiah & Esther* (Pasadena, CA:Thru The Bible Books, 1977), p. 192.

100. Rabbi Nisson Wolpin, Editor, *Seasons of the Soul*, (Israel: Mesorah Publications Ltd., 1981,), p. 171.

101. David C. Gross, *The Jewish People's Almanac* (NY: Hippocrene Books Inc. 1988), p. 188.

102. McGee, op. cit. p. 248.

103. Wolpin, op. cit. p. 182.

104. Josephus, op. cit. p. 324

105. Bloch, op. cit., p. 51.

106. Arnold G. Fruchtenbaum, *The Feast of Channukah* (Tustin, CA: Ariel Ministries, 1987), p. 4.

107. Arthur W, Pink, *Exposition of The Gospel of John*, (Grand Rapids, MI: Zondervan Publishing, 1975), p. 544.

108. *Scofield Reference Bible*, op. cit. Daniel 11:35, footnote 1.

109. Charles J. Woodbridge, *Bible Prophecy* (Chicago: Moody Bible Institute 1962), p. 23.

110. Dwight J. Pentecost, *Things To Come* (Dunham Publishing Company, 1958/ Grand Rapids, MI: Zondervan Publishing Company, 1978), p. 229.

111. All New Testament thief verses. Matthew 24:43, 26:55; Mark 14:48; Luke 12:33, 39, 22:52; John 10:1, 10, 12:6; I Thessalonians 5:2, 4; I Peter 4:15; II Peter 3:10; Revelation 3:3, 16:15.

112. Harry A. Ironside, *Matthew* (Neptune, NJ: Loizeaux Brothers, 1948), p. 316.

113. Arno C. Gaebelein, *The Gospel Of Matthew* (Neptune, NJ: Loizeaux Brothers, 1961), p. 511.

114. John F. Walvoord, *Matthew—Thy Kingdom Come* (Chicago: Moody Press, 1974), pp. 181, 191.

115. J. Vernon McGee, *Matthew* (Pasadena, CA: Thru The Bible Radio, 1973), vol. 2., p. 105.

116. John F. Walvoord, *The Rapture Question* (Grand Rapids, MI: Zondervan Publishing House, 1979), p. 189.

117. J. Vernon McGee, *Mark* (Pasadena, CA: Thru The Bible Books, 1975), p. 150.

118. J.A. MacDonald, *The Pulpit Commentary* (Peabody MA: Hendrickson Publishers), vol. XV pp. 463-464.

119. J.D.Douglas, op. cit., p. 856.

120. Donald Grey Barnhouse, *Genesis* (Grand Rapids, MI: Zondervan Publishing House, 1970), p. 30.

121. J. Vernon McGee, *Hebrews* (Pasadena, CA: Thru The Bible Books, 1978), vol. II p. 46.
     The Pulpit Commentary (Peabody, MA: Hendrickson Publishers), vol. XXI pp.241, 250, 262 and vol. XV p. 464
     John F. Walvoord, *Matthew—Thy Kingdom Come* (Chicago: Moody Press, 1974), pp. 191-104.

122. *Jerusalem Post*, (February 16, 1991), [Sanhedrin 97b].

123. J. Vernon McGee, *Daniel* (Pasadena, CA: Thru The Bible Books, 1978), pp. 156.